intermediate

workbook
Innovations

a course in natural English

Hugh Dellar and Andrew Walkley

THOMSON
™

United Kingdom • United States • Australia • Canada • Mexico • Singapore • Spain

Innovations Intermediate Workbook
Hugh Dellar and Andrew Walkley

Publisher: *Christopher Wenger*
Series Editor: *Jimmie Hill*
Editorial Manager: *Howard Middle/HM ELT Services*
Director of ESL/ELT Development: *Anita Raducanu*
Director of Marketing, ESL/ELT: *Amy Mabley*
Developmental Editor: *Paul MacIntyre*
Sr. Production Editor: *Sally Cogliano*
Sr. Print Buyer: *Mary Beth Hennebury*
Associate Marketing Manager: *Laura Needham*

Compositor: *Process ELT (www.process-elt.com)*
Production Management: *Process ELT*
Illustrator: *Peter Standley*
Photography Manager: *Sheri Blaney*
Photo Researcher: *Process ELT*
Copyeditor: *Process ELT*
Cover/Text Designer: *Studio Image & Photographic Art (www.studio-image.com)*

Printer: Webcom

Printed in Canada
4 5 6 7 8 9 10 08 07

For more information contact Thomson Learning, High Holborn House, 50/51 Bedford Row, London WC1R 4LR United Kingdom or Heinle, 25 Thomson Place, Boston, Massachusetts 02210 USA. You can visit our Web site at http://www.heinle.com

For permission to use material from this text or product contact us:
Tel   1-800-730-2214
Fax   1-800-730-2215
Web   www.thomsonrights.com

ISBN-13: 978-0-7593-9845-0
ISBN-10: 0-7593-9845-3
Workbook

Photo Credits

Page 14 © Image Source Limited/Index Stock Imagery
Page 22 © Pixland/Index Stock Imagery
Page 23 © Digital Vision/Picture Quest
Page 25 © Tom Carroll/Index Stock Imagery
Page 59 © Benelux Press/Index Stock Imagery

To the student

Studying on your own outside class is just as important as the work you do in class with your teacher. Learning a language is not something which happens immediately or when you want it to happen! Learning takes time. You can make the process faster and more efficient if you study at home.

This Workbook has been specially designed to make sure you really learn how to use the language you meet in class. It gives you more opportunities to practise grammar, it helps you check your understanding of how to use new vocabulary in typical, everyday ways and it helps you develop your written English, too.

Here is some general advice for how to get the most out of this book:

- Do a little every day rather than a lot once a week.
- Try to do the exercises first without using the answer key, but don't be afraid to use the answer key, if you have a problem.
- Look back at earlier units in the book after you have finished them. It is important to make sure you remember what you have already studied. Sometimes, just re-reading exercises you did a few weeks before can help you to remember things.
- Before you start working on your own, study the exercises on page 7.

Contents

Introduction	7		
		1	What is a collocation?
		2	Making the most of your study time
		3	Grammar

Unit 1
Getting to know you — 8

1	Do you like … ?	6	Collocations with *question* and *answer*
2	How old are they?	7	Classroom language
3	Where is it?	8	Past simple and past continuous
4	What's your city like?	9	Writing: an anecdote
5	Collocations with *heavy*		

Unit 2
Free time — 12

1	I just stayed in and had an early night	7	What kind of thing is it?
2	Common answers	8	How long have you been doing that, then?
3	Where do you do that, then?	9	Past simple questions with *How long?*
4	Expressions of time	10	Asking questions using auxiliary verbs
5	How did you get into that?		
6	What's the activity?		

Unit 3
Holidays — 16

1	Free time	6	Answering *Have you been to … ?*
2	Go + -ing	7	Present perfect and adverbs
3	Collocations: *travel, trip, holiday*	8	I've just told you!
4	Whereabouts are you going?	9	Supposed to be
5	Talking about places	10	Writing: a postcard

Unit 4
Feelings — 20

1	Starting conversations	7	Adjectives with two forms
2	How's it going?	8	Present continuous: negative responses
3	Ending conversations	9	Using the present continuous
4	Social problems	10	Explaining present states
5	More expressions with *get*	11	In the middle of
6	I was surprised!		

Unit 5
Work — 24

1	What do you do?	6	Looking for something else
2	Abbreviations	7	Must be, must get
3	Have to, don't have to, can	8	Work collocations
4	I could never get used to that	9	Writing: a covering letter
5	Conversations about jobs		

Unit 6
Shopping — 28

1	Shopping collocations	5	So and such
2	The best thing is …	6	Time is money
3	Do you know if there's a chemist's near here?	7	Problems in shops
4	So do I / Neither do I	8	Things we say in shops
		9	Supposed to

Unit 7
Complaints — 32

1	Things we say in hotels	6	Excuses
2	Problems in restaurants	7	It really gets on my nerves!
3	Not very good	8	More problems
4	Commenting on what people say	9	Writing: a letter of complaint
5	Had to, didn't have to	10	Using the passive

Unit 8
House and home — 36

1	Who do you live with?	6	Describing areas 2
2	What's your flat like?	7	Describing people's bad habits
3	Was it very expensive?	8	Housework
4	Describing trends	9	Collocations with *home* or *house*
5	Describing areas 1	10	Asking for permission and making requests

Unit 9
Computers 40

1 Your computer
2 Talking about computers
3 What software do you use?
4 Computers – love them or hate them?
5 Have you ever … ?
6 Superlatives with the present perfect
7 Replying to advice
8 Responding to advice
9 Keep + -ing
10 Collocations with *mistake*
11 Writing: e-mails

Unit 10
Meeting people 44

1 Sorry I'm late
2 Keyword: *main*
3 Using the infinitive to express purpose
4 A night out
5 Arranging to meet
6 I'm just phoning to …
7 I'm not bothered
8 Adding extra comments
9 Verb patterns
10 Do you want to … , or shall we … ?

Unit 11
Transport and travel 48

1 Cars
2 Tend to
3 How did it happen?
4 Comparing now with the past
5 Fixed comparative phrases
6 More comparatives
7 Nightmare journeys
8 Collocations with *rough*
9 What a stupid thing to do!
10 Writing: connecting ideas

Unit 12
Food 52

1 It's a kind of …
2 *Too* and *enough*
3 There's too much / There are too many
4 Keyword: *food*
5 Food vocabulary
6 It should be banned
7 Eating vocabulary
8 Eating out in a big group
9 More questions you might ask in a group
10 Should've / shouldn't have

Unit 13
Sightseeing 56

1 Places to visit
2 What's it like?
3 Questions and answers
4 Weather vocabulary
5 I don't know
6 'll / going to / might
7 Future expressions
8 I might … if …
9 It depends
10 Writing: I was wondering

Unit 14
Studying 60

1 School subjects
2 The worst teacher I ever had!
3 Punishments
4 Verb patterns
5 How did your exam go?
6 How did it go?
7 Studying at university
8 What are you studying?
9 Tests and exams
10 Plans and hopes
11 Short natural answers

Unit 15
Sport 64

1 *Do, play* or *go*?
2 Are you any good?
3 *Win* or *beat*?
4 Different kinds of games
5 More first conditionals
6 Expressions with *if*
7 He should've scored that!
8 I know / I don't know
9 Writing

Unit 16
Business 68

1 What kind of business?
2 Problems, problems!
3 More problems
4 Collocations: *company* and *business*
5 How's business?
6 Business verbs
7 Important expressions
8 Promises, promises!
9 First and second conditionals
10 Grammar: *would* or *'ll*

Unit 17
Friends and family   72

1 Relationships
2 Adjectives and expressions to describe people
3 Know, get to know, meet, make, have
4 Present perfect and past simple
5 Relationship verbs
6 Second conditionals
7 Guessing and being vague
8 Talking about recent history
9 I used to, but I don't any more
10 Writing: describing social trends

Unit 18
Nationalities, festivals and languages   76

1 Festivals
2 Reacting to good and bad news
3 Relative clauses
4 Relative clauses in questions
5 Language and speakers
6 Talking about language
7 Superlatives
8 Countries and nationalities
9 Describing your country
10 Where's that, then?

Unit 19
Law and order   80

1 Different kinds of crimes
2 Punishments
3 Number expressions
4 Basic crime vocabulary
5 Famous and dangerous!
6 Keyword: crime
7 Third conditionals 1
8 Third conditionals 2
9 I wish I'd … / I wish I hadn't
10 Writing

Unit 20
Health   84

1 Health problems
2 What's the matter?
3 Being ironic
4 I'm allergic to it
5 Health vocabulary
6 Things doctors say
7 How did you do that, then?
8 Reporting speech 1
9 Reporting speech 2
10 Keyword: health
11 Giving advice
12 Should for talking about the future

Answer Key   88

Introduction

The main goal of the *Innovations* series is to help you speak English fluently and understand spoken English. Because of this, most of the exercises in this book give spoken models of how the language is normally used. One of the most important things to think about when studying English on your own is collocation.

1 | What is a collocation?

A collocation is two or more words which often go together. This often means an adjective + a noun, a verb + a noun or a noun + a noun. Some of the exercises in this Workbook look at collocations of common words – *question, answer, get, go* – because we believe it is important to learn how to use these useful words in lots of different ways.

Underline the useful collocations in these sentences. The first one is done for you.

1. My grandfather is eighty-seven now. He's starting to lose his memory.
2. Shall we leave a tip?
3. My brother left home recently.
4. Sorry I'm late. I overslept and missed my train.
5. I'm going on holiday in two weeks.
6. My son is doing a degree in Liverpool.
7. It's a part-time course – two days a week for ten weeks.
8. Can you save my seat, please? I'll be back soon.
9. My parents got divorced when I was six or seven.
10. I don't feel very well. I've got an upset stomach.

Learning new collocations is a big part of learning a language. One thing this means for you is that you need to be careful when translating into your own language. It is always better to translate collocations – or even whole sentences – rather than single words.

2 | Making the most of your study time

Translating from English into your own language is normal at this level. We think that when you study this Workbook at home, it is a good idea to also keep your own vocabulary notebook, where you write down new bits of English on the left and translations on the right. Here is an exercise which shows you how to get the most from translation.

Start your vocabulary notebook by writing the sentences 1–10 below on a page. Write a translation beside each expression in your own language. In one week's time, test yourself by covering 1–10 and using your translations to help you remember the whole sentences in English.

1. Unemployment is very high at the moment.
2. I'd like to make a complaint.
3. I hope the weather is OK this weekend.
4. Can we get the bill, please?
5. I had my bag stolen.
6. There's a film on later I'd like to watch.
7. Have you had any lunch?
8. There were hardly any people there.
9. My flight leaves at seven thirty in the morning.
10. It usually takes me about twenty minutes.

3 | Grammar

This Workbook gives you plenty of chances to look at the most common, useful grammatical structures in English. You will look at how to form these structures and also how to use them in everyday contexts.

Here is a list of some common grammatical terms used in this book. Match the terms 1–8 to the underlined examples in the sentences a–h.

1. past simple ☐
2. present continuous ☐
3. past continuous ☐
4. comparative adjectives ☐
5. present perfect simple ☐
6. a superlative adjective ☐
7. present perfect continuous ☐
8. reported speech ☐

a. I was living in Norway at the time.
b. Have you ever been to Peru?
c. It's much nicer – and it's cheaper too.
d. We rented a car for a few days.
e. It's the biggest place in town.
f. He told me to stay at home and take it easy.
g. How long have you been studying English?
h. I'm reading a great book at the moment.

1 Getting to know you

1 Do you like ...?

Complete the short dialogues below with the answers in the box.

> It's all right, I suppose   No, not really
> I've never heard of them   Yeah, I love it
> No, I hate him   Yeah, they're OK

1. A: Do you like football?
   B: .... It's one of my favourite sports. What about you?

2. A: Do you like Leonardo di Caprio?
   B: .... ! I really don't understand why so many people like him so much! Why? Do you like him?

3. A: Do you like reading?
   B: .... I much prefer watching movies or listening to music. What about you?

4. A: Do you like The Thirteenth Floor Elevators?
   B: .... What kind of music do they play?

5. A: Do you like shopping?
   B: .... I don't mind it, but I'm not crazy about it. What about you?

6. A: Do you like the people you work with?
   B: .... We get on all right, I suppose. What about you?

Now match the comments a–f to the questions at the end of the dialogues 1–6 above.

a. Oh, I'm crazy about it too. I play quite a lot, actually. That's why I asked. ☐

b. Oh, I love it. I'm especially keen on books about history. ☐

c. Yeah, I love him. He's really good-looking and he can act as well! ☐

d. Yeah, they're great. We all get on really well. ☐

e. Oh, I'm the same as you about it. I can take it or leave it. ☐

f. They're quite hard to describe, actually. You'd have to hear them! ☐

2 How old are they?

Match the ages 1–5 to the more general expressions a–e.

1. She's only two weeks old. ☐
2. She's nearly two years old now. ☐
3. She's nine. ☐
4. She's fifteen. ☐
5. She's twenty-one. ☐

a. She's an adult.
b. She's a child.
c. She's a teenager.
d. She's a baby.
e. She's a toddler.

Now match the ages 6–10 to the more general expressions f–j.

6. He's twenty-eight. ☐
7. He's thirty-six. ☐
8. He's forty-two. ☐
9. He's fifty-one. ☐
10. He's seventy-nine. ☐

f. He's quite elderly now.
g. He's in his late twenties.
h. He's middle-aged.
i. He's in his mid-thirties.
j. He's in his early forties.

> **Language note**
>
> If we say 'She's old', it can sound rude or cold. If we want to sound nicer, we usually say 'She's quite elderly'. You might sometimes hear people say 'She's getting on a bit now'. This is a slightly more friendly, informal way of saying the same thing.

3 Where is it?

Look at the pairs of sentences below and decide which sentence (a or b) matches the picture.

1.

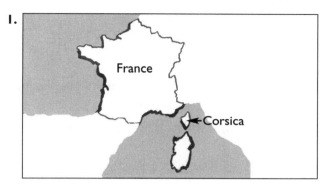

a. It's on the south coast.
b. It's off the south coast.

2.

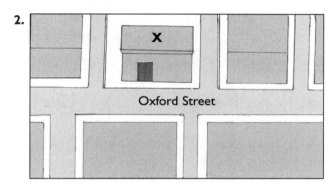

a. It's on Oxford Street.
b. It's off Oxford Street.

3.

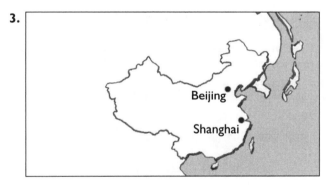

a. It's in south Beijing.
b. It's south of Beijing.

4.

a. It's an area in the west of Madrid.
b. It's a place just west of Madrid.

Make sentences by matching the beginnings 5–9 to the endings a–e.

5. It's right in the city centre, ☐
6. It's right next to the sea, ☐
7. It's right in the middle of England, ☐
8. It's right out in the country, ☐
9. It's right opposite a park with some tennis courts, ☐

a. so we go swimming most days. It's lovely.
b. so I walk everywhere.
c. so it's easy to travel round the country.
d. so we play nearly every day in the summer.
e. so it takes ages to get into town every day for work.

4 What's your city like?

Match the answers 1–5 to the follow-up comments a–e.

1. It's nice. It's a famous old city. ☐
2. It's nice. It's a big seaside resort. ☐
3. It's nice. It's a very cosmopolitan place. ☐
4. It's OK, but it's quite polluted. ☐
5. It's nice. It's a very modern city. ☐

a. It's really lively in the summer, but it's dead in the winter.
b. It's got a really good new transport system, so it's easy to get round.
c. The traffic's really heavy, especially during rush hour.
d. The centre dates back more than six hundred years.
e. There are people from all over the world there.

Now match the answers 6–10 to the follow-up comments f–j.

6. It's OK, but the climate's horrible. ☐
7. It's OK. It's a big commercial centre. ☐
8. It's OK, but it's very small. ☐
9. It's not very nice. It's a big industrial city. ☐
10. It's not that nice. It's a big port. ☐

f. All the ferries to the islands leave from there.
g. It's freezing in the winter and it's really hot and humid in the summer.
h. There's nothing much to do there. I left to go to university.
i. A lot of big companies and banks have their offices there.
j. Toyota have a big car plant there.

5 | Collocations with *heavy*

In Exercise 4, you met the collocation 'The traffic's really heavy'. Complete the sentences below with the words in the box.

atmosphere	sleeper
conversation	smoker
film	suitcases
lunch	traffic
night	week

1. I'd leave now, if I were you, before the rush hour. The . . . . shouldn't be too heavy.

2. I'm a really heavy . . . . I could sleep through an earthquake!

3. He's a really heavy . . . . He's going to end up with cancer, if he doesn't stop.

4. It was a really heavy . . . . It's all about child abuse and suicide. It's awful!

5. There's quite a heavy . . . . at work at the moment because of the re-structuring. Everyone's scared they're going to be made redundant.

6. I had a rather heavy . . . . last night, so I've got a bit of a hangover this morning.

7. I've had a really heavy . . . . I just haven't stopped working.

8. She came with three really heavy . . . . – and she's only staying five days!

9. We had quite a heavy . . . . and I ended up falling asleep during the afternoon meeting.

10. The . . . . got a bit heavy after you left. He started telling us all about his divorce.

Learning tip

When you learn a new adjective, it's important to look in a good monolingual dictionary or a dictionary of collocations to see if you can find examples of the nouns it usually collocates with. The nouns that adjectives collocate with differ from language to language. Always record them in your vocabulary book together.

6 | Collocations with *question* and *answer*

Complete these sentences with *question* or *answer*.

1. If you want to ask a personal . . . . , it's better to add 'if you don't mind me asking'.

2. The polite . . . . is 'No'!

3. Can you let me think about it and I'll give you my . . . . tomorrow?

4. You can check the . . . . in the back of the book.

5. You look like you want to ask a(n) . . . . Go on, what?

6. Have you got the . . . . yet?

7. My six-year old asked me a really awkward . . . . the other day. You know the one.

8. That's a very difficult . . . . to . . . .

9. He never gives a straight . . . . He always avoids the . . . .

10. Come on! Just . . . . the . . . . !

Can you translate the sentences above into your language?

7 | Classroom language

Complete the sentences below with the correct form of the pairs of words in the box.

borrow + catch up	rub this off + write it all down
hand-out + leave	
look through + give	toilet + break
play + compare	

1. A: Is it OK if I . . . . the board now?
   B: No, not yet! I haven't . . . . yet.

2. A: Can you . . . . the tape again, please? I didn't get everything.
   B: I'll play it in a minute. First, though, just . . . . what you heard in pairs.

3. A: Sorry, but I won't be able to come to class next Tuesday.
   B: That's OK. Thanks for telling me. Make sure you . . . . someone's notes and . . . . , though.

4. A: OK. Have you got the . . . . I gave you last lesson?

    B: Sorry. I . . . . it at home. I didn't know we were going to use it.

5. A: Can I go to the . . . . ?

    B: Can't you wait till the . . . . ? It's only ten minutes away.

6. A: For homework tonight, ... your notes from today and try to memorise what we've done. I'll . . . . you a test tomorrow.

    B: A test? No! It's not fair.

Now decide if speaker A in the dialogues above is a teacher or a student.

8 Past simple and past continuous

Choose the correct form.

1. *I took / I was taking* the rubbish out when the door *closed / was closing* behind me!

2. *I rushed / I was rushing* to a meeting and so *I forgot / I was forgetting* to take my keys.

3. *I didn't recognise / I wasn't recognising* him because *he didn't wear / he wasn't wearing* his glasses.

4. *I didn't look / I wasn't looking* where *I went / I was going* and so *I stepped / I was stepping* into a big puddle.

5. *I didn't think / I wasn't thinking* what *I did / I was doing* and so *I pressed / I was pressing* 'Delete' by mistake.

6. *I just got up / I was just getting up* and *I knocked / I was knocking* the glass over.

7. *I just walked / I was just walking* past and *I caught / I was catching* my shirt on a nail.

8. *I didn't see / I wasn't seeing* him yesterday because *he worked / he was working* from home.

9 Writing: an anecdote

When we write about something that has happened to us, we often use the following pattern:

1. **We often say what the story is generally about:**
    Something happened to me the other day which was so embarrassing.
    I saw something a few days ago, which was so funny.
    I broke my leg once. It was really painful.

2. **We usually then say when it happened:**
    It was last Monday or Tuesday.
    It was one day last week.
    It happened a few years ago, when I was eighteen.

3. **We then add where it happened and what we were doing there:**
    I was at work doing a class …
    I was in town doing some shopping …
    I was in Cancun on holiday …

4. **And the events of the story:**
    and I was giving a lecture when my mobile phone went off.
    and I was walking along the main road when this guy in front of me slipped on a banana skin.
    and I was trying to dive off this rock when I slipped and fell.

5. **Finally, we make some comment on the story:**
    I went bright red. It was terrible.
    It was just like a cartoon. I just burst out laughing.
    It was terrible. I've been scared of diving ever since.

Complete the story below with the phrases in the box.

> I thought I was going to die
>
> I was on holiday
>
> I'd never do anything like that again
>
> It happened quite a few years ago
>
> once

I almost drowned (1) . . . . It was really frightening. (2) . . . . , when I was still a student. (3) . . . . in France and I was camping with some friends by a lake. There was an old rowing boat near the camp site, and one night we thought it would be good fun to go rowing on the lake. We went across the lake and then we started to come back. Everything was fine, but then, when we were trying to change places, so one of the others could row, my friend Pete stood up and put his foot through the bottom of the boat. The boat sank in about ten seconds. I started panicking because I couldn't swim very well and I was out of my depth. (4) . . . . Luckily, we weren't far from the shore, and I only had to swim about ten metres, but I'll tell you what — (5) . . . . !

Can you find any other useful phrases in the stories on page 12 of the Coursebook which fit into the categories 1–5 above?

Now try and use the structure above and write your own story about one of the following:

a. An accident you once had.

b. Something strange that once happened to you.

c. A stupid mistake you once made.

d. Something really funny that once happened to you.

e. Something really frightening that once happened to you.

2 Free time

1 | I just stayed in and had an early night

Add *just* to these sentences to make the actions sound unimportant.

1. I didn't do much last night. I stayed in and watched TV and that was it, really.
2. I didn't eat much this morning – an apple and a piece of toast.
3. It's a small company. We only employ twelve people.
4. I'm phoning to make sure you got home OK.
5. I'm writing to say 'Thanks' for the Christmas card you sent.
6. No, thanks. I'm looking.
7. I don't know why you're getting so annoyed about it. It was a silly joke!
8. I'm driving, so could you get me a Coke, please?

Now make sentences about a quiet night in by matching the beginnings 9–14 to the endings a–f.

9. I'm just going to stay in tonight and take
10. I'm just going to stay in tonight and have
11. I'm just going to stay in tonight and watch
12. I'm just going to stay in tonight and tidy up
13. I'm just going to stay in tonight and do
14. I'm just going to stay in tonight for

a. an early night.
b. my flat a bit.
c. a few things for work.
d. it easy.
e. a change.
f. a bit of TV.

2 | Common answers

Make short dialogues by matching each question 1–5 to two of the answers a–j.

1. How often do you do that, then?
2. How long have you been doing that, then?
3. Was it very expensive?
4. Are you any good?
5. Was it any good?

a. Yeah, it cost a fortune.
b. Hardly ever nowadays, but I used to do it all the time.
c. For a couple of years or so.
d. No, I'm useless, but I have only just started doing it.
e. As often as I can. I try and do some almost every day.
f. No, it was dreadful!
g. Yeah, it was brilliant!
h. No, not at all. It was dirt cheap.
i. For ages. I started when I was really young.
j. Yeah, I am, actually. I'm one of the best in the group.

3 | Where do you do that, then?

Complete the short dialogues below with the answers in the box.

> I usually just go round the block a few times.
> It's held in a community centre near my house.
> There's a course on the edge of town that's not too expensive.
> There's a court in the park near my house.
> There's a pitch in the park near my house.
> There's a pool near the station that I go to.

1. A: I went swimming last night.
   B: Oh, right. Where do you do that, then?
   A: ....

2. A: I played football with some friends of mine last night.
   B: Oh, right. Where do you do that, then?
   A: ....

3. A: I played basketball with some friends of mine last night.
   B: Oh, right. Where do you do that, then?
   A: ....

4. A: I played golf with a friend of mine last Saturday.

B: Oh, right. Where do you do that, then?

A: ....

5. A: I went jogging last night.

B: Oh, right. Where do you do that, then?

A: ....

6. A: I went to my yoga class last night.

B: Oh, right. Where do you do that, then?

A: ....

We often do sports activities in a sports centre. Match the verbs 7–12 to the words a–f to make six activities you can do in a sports centre.

7. have	☐	a.	weights
8. play	☐	b.	the running machines
9. go	☐	c.	squash
10. lift	☐	d.	swimming
11. use	☐	e.	aerobics
12. do	☐	f.	a sauna

4 Expressions of time

Make time expressions by putting the words into the correct order.

1. university / I / was / at / when

....

2. was / I / at / when / secondary / school

....

3. was / about / when / I / or / five / four

....

4. I / at / when / primary / school / was

....

5. still / I / was / a / when / baby

....

6. not / after / I / graduated / long

....

7. when / with / second / pregnant / our / was / child / I

....

8. when / studying / I / was / to / to / university / go

....

9. I / married / about / was / thirty / when / long / after / not / got / we

....

Now put the expressions 1–9 above into the order they happen. The first one is done for you.

The order is: 5, …, …, …, …, …, …, and … .

5 How did you get into that?

Match the beginnings 1–7 to the endings a–g to make answers to the question 'How did you get into that?'

1. <u>When I was at school</u>, I was in the handball team ☐

2. My auntie gave me a set of stamps when I was thirteen, and I really loved them, ☐

3. When I was living in Madrid, not long after I graduated, there were some courts near my house, ☐

4. I used to play quite a lot when I was younger, but I stopped. ☐

5. When I was at school, it was the 'in' thing to collect them, ☐

6. When I was on holiday in Rome one year, I saw some in a shop and I just liked the look of them, ☐

7. A friend of mine used to do climbing when I was at university, and he really loved it, ☐

a. so a friend and I just went down there one day and had a game and I loved it.

b. and I just carried on playing after I left.

c. but then when it went out of fashion, I just carried on. I'm glad I did!

d. so I just started like that and I've been collecting them ever since.

e. Then not long after I started this job, I met this guy who played a lot, and so I took it up again.

f. and so I just went with him one day and I've been doing it ever since.

g. and I've only ever bought Italian shoes since.

Now underline the time phrases that were used in 1-7. The first one is done for you.

6 What's the activity?

What do the people in 1–6 like doing in their free time?

1. swap them with people / go to fairs / buy them in auctions / buy them in specialist shops

....

2. do lengths / dive from the ten-metre board / the crawl / the breast stroke / have a sauna

....

3. go on the running machine / go on the rowing machine / do weights / do an aerobics class

....

4. be in a club / play against a computer / play in tournaments / study the latest moves

....

7 · What kind of thing is it?

Match the sentences 1–10 to the follow-up comments a–j.

1. I go riding once or twice a month. ☐
2. I'm learning tae-kwondo at the moment. ☐
3. I go to yoga classes twice a week. ☐
4. I go snow-boarding whenever I get the chance. ☐
5. I sing in a choir every Friday. ☐
6. I go roller-blading every Saturday with some friends. ☐
7. I play in a band with some friends of mine. ☐
8. I'm going to do my first bungee jump this Saturday. ☐
9. I'm learning to scuba dive at the moment. ☐
10. I've got my aerobics class tonight. ☐

a. I go to the stables just outside of town.
b. We rehearse in a studio under the railway bridge.
c. They do classes in the swimming pool near my house.
d. It's a kind of martial art, a bit like judo.
e. We practise in the local church.
f. It's really fun doing it to dance music, and we've got a great instructor too.
g. The snow was fantastic the last time I went.
h. We usually just go through the park, but sometimes we go further.
i. I really enjoy them. They help keep me really supple and fit.
j. There's a crane you can jump from down by the river!

8 · How long have you been doing that, then?

Make present perfect continuous questions by matching the beginnings 1–8 to the endings a–h.

1. How long've you been living ☐
2. How long've you been working ☐
3. How long've you been looking for ☐
4. How long've you been studying ☐
5. How long've you been playing ☐
6. How long've you been going out with ☐
7. How long've you been living with ☐
8. How long've you been going to ☐

a. that family, then?
b. the piano, then?
c. in this place, then?
d. aerobics classes, then?
e. for this company, then?
f. Arabic, then?
g. your girlfriend, then?
h. a job, then?

Language note

In everyday spoken language, it is very common to finish a question with *then*, especially when the question is asked in response to something just said to us. *Then* doesn't really have any meaning here. It is just a marker of the end of the question and also helps us sound interested. Here is an example:

A: I've got my book club tonight.
B: Oh right. How long've you been doing that, then?
A: Oh, quite a while now.

9 Past simple questions with *How long?*

Complete the short dialogues below with the pairs of words in the box.

do up / DIY	married / split up
hospital / operation	off work / temperature
learn / failed	stay / left
live / ran out of	work / job

1. A: How long did it take you to . . . . to drive?
    B: Forever! I . . . . my test the first two times, you see, and had to keep on having lessons!

2. A: How long did you . . . . at the party last night?
    B: Not much longer than you, actually. I must've . . . . at about one-ish.

3. A: How long did you . . . . in India?
    B: It was just over a year. I was going to stay for another six months, but I . . . . money.

4. A: How long did you . . . . in the pet shop, then?
    B: A couple of years, I suppose. It took me ages to find a better . . . . , you see.

5. A: How long did it take you to . . . . your house?
    B: Don't ask! The whole thing nearly led to me and wife divorcing! I never want to do any . . . . again!

6. A: How long was your brother . . . . for?
    B: About seven years, I think, but I could see he wasn't happy a long time before they finally . . . .

7. A: How long was your grandfather in . . . . for?
    B: A month altogether. They sent him home after a week, but then he had to go back in for a second . . . .

8. A: How long were you . . . . for?
    B: Nearly three weeks. I was in bed for the first fortnight with a really high . . . . It was horrible!

10 Asking questions using auxiliary verbs

We often show our interest or surprise in what someone has said by asking a question using an auxiliary verb:

A: I've been there.
B: Have you? Did you like it?
A: Don't you know who I am? I'm a film star.
B: Are you? You don't look like one to me.
A: I go swimming nearly every day.
B: Do you? You must be quite fit then.
A: I don't really like him.
B: Don't you? I thought you did.

Did you notice how we make the questions above? When do we make negative questions? When do we use do *you*?

Now see if your ideas were correct by completing the short dialogues below with the questions in the box. You will have to use some questions more than once.

Are you?	Didn't you?	Have you?
Can't you?	Do you?	Haven't you?
Did you?		

1. A: I went round to Sheila's on Saturday for a meal.
    B: . . . . What's she doing these days?

2. A: I went to that new Chinese place on Bradford Street last night.
    B: . . . . Was it any good?

3. A: I've been doing it for ages – at least five years.
    B: . . . . So you must be quite good, then.

4. A: My wife hardly ever cooks. I do nearly all the cooking.
    B: . . . . So you must be quite good, then.

5. A: I didn't go in the end.
    B: . . . . Why not?

6. A: I haven't seen it.
    B: . . . . You should go. You'd love it.

7. A: I've got tickets for the Man United–Man City game.
    B: . . . . Where did you get them? I thought they'd sold out weeks ago.

8. A: I'm thirty-four.
    B: . . . . I thought you were older.

9. A: I can't drive.
    B: . . . . I thought you could.

3 Holidays

1 Free time

In English, the time when we are not working or studying is not always called a holiday. Complete the definitions below with the words in the box.

day off	on holiday
day out	public holidays
long weekend	weekend

1. Saturday and Sunday are called the . . . . In some countries, it's Friday and Saturday.

2. Some people work six days a week, including weekends. The day you don't work is your . . . .

3. Apart from Saturday or Sunday, the government often decides that on certain days of the year, people don't have to go to work or school. These are called . . . . In Britain some are also called Bank Holidays and usually only last one day.

4. When we don't go to work or school for a period of time, we are . . . . It is usually for a week or more. You might spend this time at home, doing as little as possible!

5. If you go away to a different city for only one day, we say you went on a(n) . . . . or a day trip.

6. If you go away for three or four days, including the weekend, we would call it a(n) . . . .

2 Go + -ing

Complete the sentences below with the words in the box.

camping	sightseeing	snorkelling	swimming
shopping	skiing	surfing	trekking

1. I really like going . . . . I went right across the Gobi desert on my own last summer!

2. I really like going . . . . You can find some real bargains when you're abroad.

3. I really like going . . . . I always try and book a hotel with a good pool.

4. I really like going . . . . You can see some amazing fish sometimes if you're in the tropics.

5. I don't really like going . . . . very much. Everywhere is always so crowded and touristy.

6. I don't really like going . . . . very much. I'd much rather stay in a hotel. I miss my home comforts too much.

7. I don't really like going . . . . very much. I nearly drowned once doing it in Indonesia, and it really put me off.

8. I don't really like going . . . . very much. I fractured one of my legs doing it once, and it really put me off.

3 Collocations: *travel, trip, holiday*

The words *travel*, *trip* and *holiday* are often confused.

We only use *travel* to describe the general activity, rather than a specific journey or holiday. You can't say *I had a good travel*. *Travel* is often used as a verb:
We're travelling to Munich on the overnight train.
It is also used with another noun:
travel guide, travel agent, travel insurance

We generally use *trip* when we go out for a day for fun – a trip to the zoo – or if we go away to do a particular piece of work, for example, a business trip to Taiwan.

Holidays are always for fun. You can't go on a business holiday.

However, remember that you can't always explain why some words are used together and some aren't! The best way to learn how they are used is simply to notice and learn the typical expressions you find them in.

Complete these sentences with *travel, trip* or *holiday(s)*.

1. We went on . . . . to Germany last year.

2. We went on a day . . . . to the beach.

3. I'm on . . . . at the moment.

4. He's on a business . . . . in Birmingham.

5. I work in a . . . . agent's.

6. I need a . . . . !

7. We're going on a package . . . . to Ibiza.

8. We're going on a boat . . . . down the Nile.

9. Did you have a nice . . . . to the monastery?

10. We bought a . . . . card to use on the trains and buses.

11. May the First is a public . . . . in most countries.

12. What are you doing during the summer . . . . ?

13. We're going on a three-day hunting . . . . up into the mountains.

14. I really like to read . . . . writing.

15. It's a . . . . resort.

16. It was one of the most relaxing . . . . I've ever had.

17. We just had a beach . . . .

18. . . . . broadens the mind.

Do you agree with number 18?

4 Whereabouts are you going?

Make answers to the question above by matching the beginnings 1–10 to the endings a–j.

1. We're going to this little place in the middle ☐
2. We're staying in this small resort halfway ☐
3. We're going to fly into L.A. and then go up ☐
4. We're going to fly to Beijing and then go down ☐
5. We're going to fly to Bangkok and then backpack ☐
6. We're driving down to the south of France and staying ☐
7. We're staying in this hotel right in the ☐
8. We're staying in a cottage up in ☐
9. We're going to stay in this little place just outside ☐
10. We're going on a boating holiday along ☐

a. round the country.
b. the mountains north of Milan.
c. the coast north to San Francisco.
d. centre of Tokyo.
e. of nowhere.
f. the River Thames.
g. Athens.
h. between Barcelona and Valencia.
i. in campsites along the way.
j. the coast south to Shanghai.

5 Talking about places

Complete the sentences below with the words in the box.

capital	mountain range	stream
counties	states	wood
lake		

1. It's funny, because people always think Rio de Janeiro is the . . . . of Brazil, but it's not.

2. We went skiing in the Dolomites. They're a . . . . in the north of Italy.

3. It's a really beautiful place to stay. There's a lovely little . . . . that runs past the hotel, and then a few miles up the road there's a huge big . . . . where you can go windsurfing and water-skiing.

4. There's a nice little . . . . near our house, where I sometimes take the dog for a walk.

5. I've never understood why in America, places like Florida or Texas are called . . . . , while in Britain, places like Essex or Yorkshire are called . . . . ! It's so confusing.

Complete the sentences below with the words in the box.

cliff	hills	scenery	waterfall
forest	river	views	

6. We drove from Zagreb down to the Dalmatian coast and the . . . . along the way was amazing!

7. My uncle lives on the edge of this great big . . . . Once you go past his house, it's just trees for miles and miles.

8. If you walk along the banks of the . . . . for a mile or two, you come to this beautiful . . . . , where it drops down maybe four or five hundred metres. It's really beautiful!

9. You can walk up to the top of most of the . . . . round there in an hour or two. It's well worth the effort, because you get great . . . . of the valleys from up there.

10. It's quite a dangerous walk up there. Every year people fall off the edge of the . . . . and into the sea!

Which is bigger, …

a. a sea or an ocean? . . . .
b. a forest or a wood? . . . .
c. a mountain or a hill? . . . .
d. a sea or a lake? . . . .
e. a stream or a river? . . . .

6 | Answering: *Have you been to ...?*

Complete these answers to the question 'Have you ever been to Egypt?' Use only one word in each space.

1. No, but the scenery's .... to be amazing.
2. No, but I've always .... to.
3. Yeah, but I'm not .... I'd go again.
4. Yeah, the nightlife's brilliant. You'll .... it.
5. Yeah, I went there once .... I was at university.
6. No, but I'd love ....
7. Yeah, but it rained the .... time we were there.
8. No, but I .... never really wanted to.
9. Yeah, and it was horrible! I .... n't go there again even if you paid me.
10. No, but a friend of .... has.

7 | Present perfect and adverbs

Make short dialogues by matching the questions 1–9 to the answers a–i.

1. Do you want a coffee?
2. Do you want some more cake?
3. Do you fancy going to see that new French movie?
4. Did you know I'm changing jobs?
5. Did you know my dad died?
6. Did you know Sarah's had a baby boy?
7. Have you ever been to the Middle East?
8. Have you ever been to the Far East?
9. Have you seen that new musical yet?

a. Yeah, I've just heard. I hope you'll like it.
b. Yeah, Jane's just told me. That's awful. I am sorry.
c. No, honestly, I'm full. I've already had three pieces.
d. No, but I've never really fancied it. The twelve-hour flight puts me off.
e. No thanks. I've just had one.
f. Do you mean the one that Abba did the music for? No, do you really fancy going to see it?
g. Do you mean *Les Idiots*? I've actually seen it already.
h. No, but I've always wanted to. I'd love to see places like Cairo and Jerusalem one day.
i. Yeah. Have you seen him yet?

Underline the adverbs in a–i. Did you notice where they come in each sentence?

8 | I've just told you!

We often show that we completed something very recently by using *just* and the present perfect. For example:

A: What does this mean?
B: I've just told you! Weren't you listening?

We sometimes add *only*, *actually*, or *this second/minute* for extra emphasis. For example:

I've only just arrived here, so I don't know my way round yet.

I've actually just spoken to him this second, so if you ring him now, he'll be there.

Complete these short dialogues by putting the verbs in brackets into the present perfect with *just*.

1. A: Hi, is Joyce in?
   B: Yeah, I .... (see) her walking down the stairs. I think she was going to the canteen.

2. A: Sorry, I'm late. I got held up at work.
   B: Don't worry. I .... (only / get) here myself. I think the programme .... (only / started), so we won't have missed any of the film.

3. A: What do you do?
   B: I .... (only / graduate) from university, so nothing at the moment. I thought I'd have a holiday first.

4. A: Are you OK? You sound a bit upset.
   B: Yeah, I am a bit. I .... (find out) the holiday company we were going to travel with .... (go bankrupt), so I've lost fifteen hundred pounds, the holiday, everything!

5. A: Have you sorted out the plane tickets?
   B: I .... (do) it this minute. They said they'll be in the post tonight, so we should get them by Thursday at the latest.

6. A: Hi, it's Faten. Is Michelle back from holiday yet?
   B: She .... (actually / walk) through the door this second! I'll pass you over once she's taken her coat off.

9 Supposed to be

We use *supposed to be* when we want to report what we have read, heard or what someone else told us. For example:

That restaurant's supposed to be great. A friend of mine went there last week and he loved it.

That place is supposed to be horrible – just full of tourists. There was an article in the paper about it.

When we have actually been somewhere, we just use a form of *be* and we often tell the person about the time we went there. For example:

That restaurant's great. We went there two weeks ago. They do really good lamb dishes.

That place is horrible. I went there on a cheap package holiday last year. It was awful.

Now complete these sentences with the correct form of *be* or *be supposed to be*.

1. The place . . . . really polluted. A friend of mine told me you can only see 500 metres because of all the smoke and fumes.

2. The nightlife . . . . amazing. We were out till four in the morning most nights we were there.

3. The beaches . . . . fantastic. That's why we've decided to go and see for ourselves.

4. The countryside . . . . amazing. I saw a documentary about it and it looked beautiful.

5. The city centre . . . . quite dangerous. There was a thing on the news about it the other day.

6. There . . . . quite a lot of crime. We got mugged twice while we were there.

7. The view from the top . . . . absolutely amazing. We could see the whole of the city and beyond the day we went up there.

Now choose the more natural words in these sentences.

8. The museum's *supposed to get / gets* very busy in the afternoon. I read something about it in the guide book.

9. It's *not supposed to be / 's not* worth the entrance fee. Caroline and Dave went and they said it was quite boring.

10. It's *supposed to be / 's* a really terrible hotel. I stayed there a couple of years ago and they had rats and cockroaches in all the rooms!

11. I've never been to the Lake District, but it *is supposed to be / is* lovely.

12. I shouldn't be ringing you. I'*m supposed to be / 'm* working!

10 Writing: a postcard

Complete the postcard below with the words in the box.

architecture	having	missing	spent
couple	lying	off	staying

Dear Rachel,

(1) . . . . a really good time in Turkey.
(2) . . . . three days in Istanbul, which was amazing – great (3) . . . ., great food and a really exciting place to be. We're now in Izmir for a (4) . . . . of days, (5) . . . . with an old friend, and will shortly be (6) . . . . to Antalya for a week of (7) . . . . around on the beach, doing nothing. The weather's been great and we're not (8) . . . . grey old Faversham at all!

Hope all is well with you.

Lots of love,

Tiffany and Simon

Typical postcard language
Make sentences by matching the beginnings 1–9 to the endings a–i.

1. The weather's great, ☐
2. The weather's not wonderful ☐
3. The weather's terrible, ☐
4. The food's delicious – ☐
5. The food's not too bad – ☐
6. The food's not very good, ☐
7. The architecture's amazing, ☐
8. The beaches are amazing, ☐
9. The nightlife is amazing, ☐

a. but we're having a good time anyway.
b. but it could be worse. We could be back home!
c. so we've been doing plenty of sunbathing.
d. but we've managed to avoid food poisoning so far!
e. we've been eating out in some great places.
f. I suppose I've eaten worse!
g. so we've been busy working on our tans.
h. so we've been going out clubbing quite a lot.
i. so we've been doing lots of sightseeing.

Imagine you are on holiday now. Decide where you are and how you are spending your time. Now write a postcard to a friend of yours, telling them a bit about different things. Use the postcard above as a model to help you.

4 Feelings

1 Starting conversations

First complete these questions that we often use to start conversations.

1. All right. How's it . . . . ? ☐

2. Hiya. I'm really sorry I'm late. . . . . you been . . . . long? ☐

3. It's been ages! . . . . have you been . . . . since I last saw you? ☐

4. It's James, ... it? ☐

5. Morning. Did you sleep . . . . ? ☐

6. Did you have a . . . . weekend? ☐

7. Hello. Do you . . . . if I . . . . you? ☐

8. What're you . . . . to now? ☐

Now make short dialogues by matching the questions 1–8 above to the answers a–h.

a. No, only about ten minutes. The traffic was awful!

b. Yeah, not too bad, but I woke up very early for some reason.

c. Yeah, it was great. I went to stay with some friends who live in Bristol.

d. No, sorry. I think you must've mistaken me for someone else.

e. Nothing really. I've just been really busy with work. I did get married, though.

f. Oh, I'm just on my way home, actually. What about you?

g. Not too bad, you know. I'm surviving.

h. No, of course not. Do you want to try to get a seat from somewhere?

2 How's it going?

Here are four possible responses to the common question 'How's it going?' Match each of the responses 1–4 to three of the follow-up comments a – l.

1. I'm actually feeling a bit ill. ☐ ☐ ☐
2. I'm exhausted, to be honest. ☐ ☐ ☐
3. To be honest, I'm a bit fed up. ☐ ☐ ☐
4. Actually, I'm in a really good mood. ☐ ☐ ☐

a. I think I ate something which was off. I was up all night being sick.

b. A couple of friends came round last night and we were up till three chatting.

c. I went out last night and I think I had a bit too much to drink.

d. I think I'm getting a cold or something.

e. I didn't get that job I applied for.

f. I got a letter from this friend in America and he's coming over to see me.

g. I went to the gym yesterday and I think I overdid it.

h. I got my exam results this morning and I passed.

i. It's this weather! I'm sick of it!

j. I'm just a bit bored with what I'm doing at the moment.

k. I just couldn't get to sleep last night.

l. I met this really nice woman recently.

3 Ending conversations

We often finish conversations by saying 'Listen, I've got to go', and then giving a reason for leaving. Each of the examples 1–10 below includes a reason for ending a conversation. Put the words in brackets into the correct order.

1. Listen, I've got to go . . . .
   (I'll / or / late / be)

2. Listen, I've got to go . . . .
   (miss / or / my / I'll / train)

3. Listen, I've got to go . . . .
   (or / the / miss / I'll / the / start / film / of)

4. Listen, I've got to go . . . .
   (I / work / finish / or / this / won't)

5. Listen, I've got to go . . . .
   (husband / my / or / will / to / worry / start)

6. Listen, I've got to go. . . . .
   (cooking / boyfriend's / My / dinner)

7. Listen, I've got to go. . . . .
   (friend's / for / waiting / A / me)

8. Listen, I've got to go. . . . .
   (meeting / a / six / of / I'm / mine / friend / at)

9. Listen, I've got to go. . . . .
   (a / film / TV / There's / on / I / watch / want / to)

10. Listen, I've got to go. . . . .
    (tennis / a / There's / match / I / on / to / want / TV / watch)

Which excuse do you use most often?

4 Social problems

Which of the social problems 1–6 are being described in sentences a–f?

1. homelessness ☐
2. bullying ☐
3. drug abuse ☐
4. sexual discrimination ☐
5. organised crime ☐
6. racism ☐

a. It's terrible! It happens to kids who are too fat or who wear glasses or who don't have the right clothes. Other kids at school beat them up and put their heads down toilets – that kind of thing.

b. There's still a lot of it about. It's still much harder for women to get good jobs than it is for men, and women still earn less, too. When was the last time you met a female boss?

c. There's still a bit of racially motivated violence. Last year a young black was stabbed to death by a gang of white kids. It also means it's harder for black people to get good jobs.

d. It's a big problem in the inner cities. You get hundreds of people sleeping rough in doorways at night and then begging during the day.

e. It's big business! They control a lot of underground gambling and prostitution – that kind of thing.

f. It used to be just heroin that was the big problem, but a lot of young people now have problems with crack cocaine too. When they get addicted, they often commit crimes to help pay for it.

5 More expressions with *get*

Complete the sentences below with the words in the box.

£4.50	details	late	petrol
angry	essay	permission	stolen

1. My bicycle got . . . . last Friday! I'm really annoyed about it.

2. He's got a very short temper. He gets . . . . really easily!

3. I really should get going. It's getting really . . . . and I don't want to miss the last bus.

4. Can you keep an eye out for a garage? We need to stop and get some . . . . soon.

5. The money's terrible where I work! I only get . . . . an hour.

6. I've got to get this . . . . finished by Monday. I'll fail the course if I hand it in late.

7. We wanted to build some new offices there, but we couldn't get planning . . . . from the local government.

8. The police will probably need to get some . . . . from you about the accident.

6 I was surprised!

Match the comments 1–8 to the follow-up comments a–h.

1. I was surprised at how clean Tokyo was. ☐
2. I was surprised at how cheap Istanbul was. ☐
3. I was surprised at how easy the exam was. ☐
4. I was surprised at how cosmopolitan Oman was. ☐
5. I was surprised about the number of people living on the streets in Brighton. ☐
6. I was surprised about the number of pigeons you see everywhere in London. ☐
7. I was surprised about the amount of traffic there was in Newcastle. ☐
8. I was surprised about the amount of rubbish there was everywhere in Paris. ☐

a. There were people from lots of different cultures living there.

b. It takes forever to get anywhere, and the pollution is awful!

c. Why doesn't the government do something about it?

d. I only spent thirty pounds the whole weekend!

e. In my country, they'd catch them and eat them!

f. There wasn't any rubbish anywhere.

g. I was expecting it to be nice and clean.

h. I was expecting it to be really difficult.

Did you notice the patterns in sentences 1–8 above? Complete the following rules:

a. I was surprised at . . . . + adjective.

b. I was surprised about the . . . . of + countable noun.

c. I was surprised about the . . . . of + uncountable noun.

7 Adjectives with two forms

Choose the right adjective.

1. I was quite *disappointed / disappointing* at how badly we played.

2. It was a really *disappointed / disappointing* ending.

3. I really thought he was going to shoot me. It was really *scared / scary*!

4. I could never do anything like that. I'd be too *scared / scary* of hurting myself.

5. You didn't miss much at Dave's party. It wasn't very *excited / exciting*.

6. I'm going to have a baby! I'm so *excited / exciting* about it!

7. I've had a very *stressed-out / stressful* week! I'm really glad it's nearly over!

8. Sorry I shouted at you! I'm just a bit *stressed-out / stressful* about things at the moment.

9. Were you very *upset / upsetting* when they didn't offer you the job?

10. I don't know how you can watch programmes about divorce. I just find them too *upset / upsetting*.

8 Present continuous: negative responses

Complete these short dialogues by putting the verbs in brackets into the present continuous.

1. A: Can I change channels? There's a good film I'd like to see on Channel 4.
   B: Actually, I . . . . (watch) this. I . . . . (quite / enjoy) it.

2. A: Do you fancy coming round for dinner on Sunday?
   B: I'd love to, but I . . . . (actually / go round) to John's. It's his birthday.

3. A: What's this awful noise? Can I turn it off?
   B: No, I . . . . (listen to) that. It's Deathpunk's latest CD. It's not noise, it's genius!

4. A: Hello. I'd like to book some tickets for tonight's performance.
   B: I'm sorry, we can't take any bookings at the moment. We . . . . (have) a lot of problems with our computer.

5. A: Can you help me tidy up?
   B: Yeah, in a bit. I . . . . (just / read) the end of this book.

6. A: Will you go out with me some time?
   B: I don't think it's a good idea. I like you, but I . . . . (see) someone else.

7. A: . . . . (you go) to Tim's party tonight?
   B: No, I wasn't invited! Anyway, I . . . . (meet) this old friend of mine.

9 Using the present continuous

We often use these adverbs and adverbial phrases with the present continuous: *just, at the moment, later, still, now*.

Complete these sentences by putting the adverbs in brackets into the correct place.

1. I'm waiting for a friend. We're going out for dinner later. (just)

2. What are you doing? Do you want to get something to eat? (now)

3. I'm working really, really long hours. It's driving me mad! (at the moment).

4. I'm meeting Ashley, if you fancy coming. (later)

5. What are you doing? Are you still with the same company? (at the moment)

6. I'm trying to find a new place to live. (still)

7. What are you doing now? Are you studying? (still)

8. I'm going out, so I'll phone you when I get back home. (later)

9. We're going for a coffee over the road, if you'd like to join us. (just)

10. I'm living back with my mum and dad because I got evicted from my old place. (now)

10 Explaining present states

Complete the reasons people give for not working at the moment with the words in the box.

bankrupt	quit	re-train
break	renew	stay
fed up with	restructured	the sack
illness		

1. The company I was working for went . . . . and I lost my job.

2. The company I was working for was . . . . and they made me redundant.

3. My contract came to an end and the company I was working for didn't . . . . it.

4. I was . . . . my job, so I decided to leave and look for something else.

5. I had a long term . . . . , which meant I couldn't continue with the job I was doing. I'm on sick benefit now.

6. I was made redundant, so I decided to take a(n) . . . . from work and go travelling.

7. I had a baby and I decided to take a break from work and . . . . at home until she started school.

8. I had a few problems at work and they gave me . . . .

9. I was fed up with my job, so I decided to . . . . and go back to college and . . . .

Do you know anyone who is not working at the moment? Are any of the sentences above true for them?

11 In the middle of

Make sentences by matching the beginnings 1–5 to the endings a–e.

1. Listen, can I phone you back later? I'm in the middle of washing ☐

2. Look, I'll call you back in a while. I'm in the middle of having ☐

3. Hey, can I phone you back a bit later? I'm in the middle of watching ☐

4. I think she's quite stressed-out at the moment. She's in the middle of getting ☐

5. They're fine, but they're both in the middle of doing ☐

a. their exams.
b. something on TV.
c. my hair.
d. my dinner.
e. divorced.

Now make sentences by matching the beginnings 6–10 to the endings f–j.

6. Can we make the weekend instead? I don't like going out in the middle of ☐

7. I got woken up in the middle of ☐

8. It's strange, because the hero dies in the middle of ☐

9. My boss was going on and on and I fell asleep right in the middle of ☐

10. It was awful. I completely forgot all my words in the middle of ☐

f. the night.
g. the meeting.
h. my speech.
i. the week.
j. the film.

5 Work

1 What do you do?

Complete the names of the jobs a–i by re-arranging the letters in brackets. The first letter of each word is given.

1. I work for a multi-national drugs company as a
   a. s . . . . (aslse pre)
   b. p . . . . (roupdtc mgraane)
   c. r . . . . (searechre)

2. I work for a car company as a(n)
   d. e . . . . (eegrinen)
   e. c . . . . (rpuomcet oprgrmmaer)
   f. m . . . . (kmaternig mgraane)

3. I work for a big department store as a
   g. s . . . . (sasle ssastnait)
   h. p . . . . (rseolnnpe mgraane)
   i. s . . . . (ecritusy dgaru)

2 Abbreviations

Lots of abbreviations are commonly used in the workplace. Match the abbreviations 1–6 to the full forms.

1. IT ☐   a. administration
2. PA ☐   b. laboratory
3. rep ☐   c. curriculum vitae
4. admin ☐   d. personal assistant
5. CV ☐   e. information technology
6. lab ☐   f. representative

Now complete these sentences with the abbreviations from above.

7. A: So what do you do at the university?
   B: I work in . . . ., dealing with student enrolments and that kind of thing. What about you?
   A: Oh I'm a . . . . technician in the School of Sciences.

8. I'm thinking of looking for another job, but I'll need to update my . . . . first.

9. A: I'm sorry, what did you say you do again?
   B: Oh, I'm a . . . . to one of the partners of a firm of accountants.

10. A: I'm sorry, what did you say you do again?
    B: I'm a sales . . . . for an insurance company. I'm not surprised you forgot. It's not very interesting.

11. A: I'm thinking of leaving my job and re-training in . . . . There's no future for me in the job I'm doing now.

Have you ever thought about re-training? What in?

3 Have to, don't have to, can

Make sentences by matching the beginnings 1–6 to the endings a–f.

1. I have to deal with   ☐
2. I don't have to deal with ☐
3. I have to get up   ☐
4. I can start   ☐
5. I don't have to wear   ☐
6. I have to wear   ☐

a. this horrible yellow uniform.
b. whenever I like – within limits.
c. a suit or anything, which is nice.
d. any of the accounts. Thank goodness someone else does that.
e. at about six in the morning.
f. some very difficult customers.

Make sentences by matching the beginnings 7–12 to the endings g–l.

7. I have to do   ☐
8. I can take   ☐
9. I don't usually have to meet ☐
10. I can do   ☐
11. I often have to take   ☐
12. I have to meet   ☐

g. the day off more or less whenever I want.
h. work home with me.
i. very tight deadlines sometimes.
j. clients.
k. a lot of paperwork, which I hate!
l. overtime if I need the money.

4 | I could never get used to that

Match the sentences 1–8 to the follow-up comments a–h.

1. I could never get used to being self-employed. ☐
2. I could never get used to working nine to five. ☐
3. I could never get used to working with computers. ☐
4. I could never get used to working a twelve-hour day. ☐
5. I could never get used to working from home. ☐
6. I could never get used to working in a factory. ☐
7. I could never get used to working with my hands. ☐
8. I could never get used to being unemployed. ☐

a. I'm much too clumsy! I'm sure I'd end up breaking lots of things.

b. I just can't imagine doing a forty-hour week. It'd drive me mad, that kind of typical office job.

c. I guess it might be fun to begin with, but having no money would drive me mad in the end.

d. It'd drive me mad, all that noise and dirt and all that machinery!

e. It'd drive me mad, not having people around to talk to.

f. Imagine how tired you'd be by the time you finally got home every night!

g. I'm much too disorganised to be my own boss!

h. I don't know the first thing about them. I'm useless with technology!

5 | Conversations about jobs

Put the conversations into the correct order.

Conversation 1

a. Basically, I design web sites and create new services you can access by mobile phones. ☐
b. I'm an information architect. ☐
c. What do you do? ☐
d. Oh yeah? What does that involve? ☐

Conversation 2

a. Really good. That's the main reason I'm still doing it. Hopefully, I'll be able to retire soon! ☐
b. Do you enjoy it? ☐
c. Oh, right. So, what's the money like? ☐
d. It's OK, I suppose, but the hours are really bad and it's quite stressful. ☐

Conversation 3

a. Do you enjoy your job? ☐
b. What are the other people you work with like? ☐
c. Well, there's only three of us in the office, but we get on really well. ☐
d. Yeah, it's OK, I suppose. The money's not that great, but it pays the bills. ☐

Conversation 4

a. You're joking. You must get exhausted. ☐
b. No, I love it. It's hard, but it's just really rewarding. I wouldn't do anything else. ☐
c. They are fairly bad. I'm sometimes on call for fourteen hours and I often work a six-day week. ☐
d. Sometimes, I suppose, but you get used to it. ☐
e. Do you ever think about changing jobs? ☐
f. What are the hours like where you work? ☐

Now cover the conversations above. Complete the questions below and then translate them into your language.

1. . . . . you do?
2. What does that . . . . ?
3. . . . . the money . . . . ?
4. . . . . the hours . . . . ?
5. . . . . the other people . . . . ?
6. Do you ever think about . . . . ?

Language note

The people you work with are your *colleagues* (usually in an office or professional situation) or your *workmates* (usually in a factory situation).

6 Looking for something else

Complete the sentences below with the comparative phrases in the box.

better paid	less stressful	more flexible
less repetitive	more challenging	more rewarding

1. It's got a bit boring. I don't even need to think when I'm at work any more. I need something a bit

   . . . .

2. I spend all day making rich people even richer. I need to do something . . . . , like teaching.

3. I have to do the same thing day in, day out. I could do with something a little . . . .

4. I only get six pounds an hour. I need to get something which is . . . .

5. I'm finding it really difficult to keep up with all the deadlines. I could do with something a bit

   . . . .

6. They won't let me change my hours to fit in with my children. I need something . . . .

7 Must be, must get

Put the adjectives into the correct group.

annoying	frustrated	stressful
bored	great	tiring
depressed	rewarding	upsetting
fed up		

a. That must be really . . . ./ . . . ./ . . . ./

   . . . ./ . . . ./ . . . .

b. You must get really . . . ./ . . . ./ . . . ./

   . . . .

Now complete the short dialogues below with the expressions in the box. You will need to use some more than once.

I do	No, not really
I do sometimes	That must be
it can be	You must get
it is	

1. A: We often have to meet really tight deadlines, so we sometimes work all night.

   B: Really? . . . . really stressful.

   A: Believe me, ...! That's why I'm going grey! I'll probably have a heart attack before I'm forty!

2. A: I'm a family lawyer, you know. I deal with people getting divorced and things like that.

   B: Really? . . . . quite depressing, dealing with all those failed marriages.

   A: I suppose . . . . , but you just get used to it. As soon as I leave the office, I just forget about my job.

3. A: Sometimes I teach them a word and then someone will ask me what it means two minutes later.

   B: Really? . . . . really fed up.

   A: Believe me, ...! I'm tearing my hair out most of the time!

4. A: I teach kids with learning difficulties.

   B: Really? . . . . really rewarding.

   A: Yeah, ... , I suppose, but it's actually quite frustrating too. Sometimes it's difficult to see any real improvement.

5. A: . . . . a bit bored, just being stuck in an office all day.

   B: . . . . The job's actually quite interesting and I get on really well with the other people I work with.

6. A: You must travel a lot in your job.

   B: Yeah, ... , but these days I do a lot of business through video conferences and the Internet, so I don't go away as often as I used to.

8 Work collocations

Match the sets of words 1–4 to the nouns they collocate with a–d.

1. apply for / get / look around for ☐
2. leave / be sick of / get sacked from ☐
3. write / send out / update ☐
4. a design / an electronics / an insurance ☐

a. my CV

b. my job

c. company

d. a job

Now match the verbs 5–8 to the sets of words they collocate with e–h.

5. get ☐

6. do ☐

7. work ☐

8. cut ☐

e. paperwork / the accounts / a cleaning job

f. our pay / fifty jobs / production

g. a pay rise / a Christmas bonus / a pay cut / a company car / promoted

h. from home / late / weekends / in shifts

9 Writing: a covering letter

Read the letter below written by a Spanish woman who is looking for part-time work in a shop. She is sending the letter, along with her CV, to a number of different places.

Complete the letter below with the words and expressions in the box.

as	part-time
contact	reliable
doing	sole charge
fit in with	vacancies
knowledge	various

Dear Sir/Madam,

I am writing to enquire about any possible (1) . . . . you may have at your store. I am currently studying English here in London and I would like to work (2) . . . . to allow me to continue my studies.

(3) . . . . you can see from my CV, I have several years' experience working in (4) . . . . shops in my home country. I have worked in both ladies' fashion and perfume departments (5) . . . . cashier work. For six months, I was in (6) . . . . of the record department of a large store. I have a diploma in retail management and I also have (7) . . . . of several computer programmes. I am a good, (8) . . . . worker, and I have a friendly, open manner with customers and other staff.

I would ideally like to work afternoons or evenings to (9) . . . . my studies, but I may be able to change classes if necessary.

You can (10) . . . . me on my mobile: 08769 578234, or at home on 020 889 7765. Thank you for your time, and I hope to hear from you shortly.

Yours faithfully,

Lucia Hernandez

Now match the sentence starters 11–17 to the groups of common endings a–f.

11. I have a first class degree in ☐

12. I have a diploma in ☐

13. I have some experience managing ☐

14. I have several years experience working in ☐

15. I have previous experience working with ☐

16. I would ideally like to work ☐

17. You can contact me ☐

a. projects / junior staff / a shop.

b. business management / French / history.

c. children / computers / disabled people.

d. part-time / full-time / evenings.

e. at the above address / by e-mail.

f. marketing / retail / restaurants.

g. catering / nursing / book-keeping.

Write a similar covering letter to apply for one of the following:

- work in one of the best restaurants in town
- work on a children's holiday camp or play scheme
- work for a design company

6 Shopping

1 Shopping collocations

Put these nouns in the correct group below.

brand	market	shop
business	product	

1. . . . .
   the world's leading –, a top –, the supermarket's own –, my favourite –
2. . . . .
   a profitable –, a retail –, a wholesale –, the family –, a catering –, my own –
3. . . . .
   a street –, an antiques –, a cattle –, a fish –, a fruit and vegetable –
4. . . . .
   a corner –, a pet –, a betting –, a specialist –, a second-hand –, the village –
5. . . . .
   a good –, an innovative –, a quality –, dairy –s, a very high-tech –, beauty –s

Now complete these sentences with words from above.

6. If I'm buying things like beans or soup, I always go for the supermarket's . . . . brand. It's much cheaper!

7. I always wear Levi's. They're my . . . . brand of jeans by a long way.

8. I think my dad is expecting me to take over the running of the . . . . business once he retires.

9. He's managed to turn a business that was going nowhere into a very . . . . one that now makes a lot of money.

10. I got these shoes really cheap from a second-hand stall in that big . . . . market near the station.

11. There's a great . . . . and . . . . market near my house where I do most of my food shopping.

12. My granddad's a terrible gambler. He more or less lives in the local . . . . shop!

13. I need to pop into the . . . . shop on my way home and buy food for my cat.

14. My brother's a vegan, so he doesn't eat any . . . . products at all – no milk or cheese or anything like that!

15. It's the latest gadget from Japan – a very small, very expensive and very . . . . product!

2 The best thing is ...

Make sentences by matching the common sentence starters 1–6 to the endings a–f.

1. The annoying thing about shopping with him is the fact that ☐
2. The nice thing about him is the fact that ☐
3. The great thing about camping is the fact that ☐
4. The only bad thing about the house is the fact that ☐
5. The pleasing thing about the talk was the fact that ☐
6. The amazing thing about his English is the fact that ☐

a. he's only been learning it for six months.
b. you're out in the open air and so close to nature.
c. he doesn't even try to show an interest in what I try on.
d. the area we live in is a bit rough.
e. he always takes an interest in what I've been doing.
f. lots of people asked me questions, so they were obviously interested in what I was saying

Now make sentences by matching the common sentence starters 7–11 to the endings g–k.

7. The thing that really irritates me about that shop is the fact that ☐
8. The thing that drives me mad about English is the fact that ☐
9. The thing I can't stand about him is the fact that ☐
10. The thing that really concerns me about my father is the fact that ☐
11. The thing that really bothers me about London is the fact that ☐

g. there are so many words to learn.
h. he keeps forgetting things. I'm worried he might be seriously ill.
i. you see so many homeless people on the street. Why isn't the government doing something about it?
j. they're always changing everything around, so you can never find anything.
k. he never ever listens to what you say. It's so annoying!

3 Do you know if there's a chemist's near here?

Which shops are being described below?

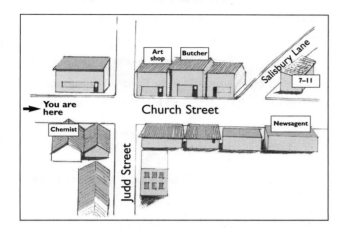

1. It's about halfway down Church Street. ....
2. It's on Salisbury Lane, just off Church Street. ....
3. It's at this end of Church Street. ....
4. It's at the end of Church Street. ....
5. It's on the corner of Church Street and Judd Street. ....

Which shops are being described below?

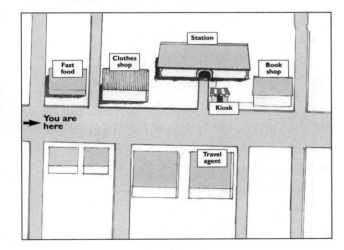

6. It's on the left, just past the station. ....
7. It's just before you get to the station. ....
8. There's one just outside the station. ....
9. It's right opposite the station. ....
10. It's on the left, about two hundred metres before the station. ....

4 So do I / Neither do I

If you agree with a positive sentence you say:
So + do / am / can / have + I. For example:

A: I love shopping
B: *So do I.* It's really good fun.

A: I'm getting the five to.
B: *So am I.* See you on the train, then.

If you agree with a negative statement you say:
Neither + do / am / can / have + I. For example:

A: I can't drive.
B: *Neither can I.* I've failed my driving test five times!

A: I didn't pay to get in.
B: *Neither did I.* I know the guy on the door as well!

Agree with these statements using the patterns above.

1. A: I really like that shop.
   B: .... It's really cheap, isn't it?
2. A: I don't like that shop.
   B: No, ... You can never find what you want.
3. A: I can't swim very well.
   B: .... I'm scared of water.
4. A: I hate that song.
   B: Yeah, ... It's really annoying because I can't stop singing it!
5. A: I'm really fed up with this weather.
   B: Yeah, ... It's just so hot I don't feel like doing anything.
6. A: I still haven't seen that new Bob Jones film.
   B: No, ... Do you want to go with me and see it next week some time?
7. A: I haven't done my homework.
   B: .... I was hoping you could give me the answers.
8. A: I've got an appointment at the dentist next week.
   B: Yeah? .... I'm dreading it.

Language note

If you disagree with or are surprised by a positive statement, you say: *Do / Are / Can / Have you?* For example:

A: I love this record.

B: Do you? I hate it. It's so sentimental and soppy.

If you disagree with or are surprised by a negative statement, you say: *Don't / Aren't / Can't / Haven't you?* For example:

A: I haven't seen *Titanic*.

B: Haven't you? I thought everybody had!

5 | *So* and *such*

Complete with *so* or *such*.

1. . . . . expensive
2. . . . . a waste of money
3. . . . . a wide choice
4. . . . . unreliable
5. . . . . friendly staff
6. . . . . cheap
7. . . . . a nice place to shop
8. . . . . dirty
9. . . . . tight
10. . . . . good value for money

Now complete the following rules:

a. If we want to make an adjective sound stronger, we can do it by putting . . . . before the adjective.

b. If we want to make an adjective + noun collocation stronger, we can do it by putting . . . . before the adjective.

Complete these sentences with words from 1–10 above.

11. This bag's really good quality, and it's so . . . . as well – only £15! I can't believe it!

12. It's a nice bag, but it's so . . . . ! I can't afford to spend £300 on something like that!

13. I love that restaurant. The food's, great and it's such . . . . , too. I mean, ten dollars for all you can eat!

14. It's a nice cafe, and they've got such . . . . , too. I always leave them a tip when I go there.

15. I like it, but because it's second-hand it's just so . . . . I mean, look at the mark on the sleeve there!

16. I don't know how you can breathe in that skirt! It looks so . . . . I'm amazed you got it on!

17. That new mall is such . . . . It's so bright and open, and you've got everything you want under one roof, too.

18. I prefer Oddbins, to be honest. They've got such . . . . of wines and beers. They're great.

19. I'd never buy any British electrical goods. They're so . . . . – they'd break within a month or two.

20. I can't believe he paid eight hundred dollars for that belt. It's such . . . . ! He must be mad!

6 | Time is money

Complete each pair of sentences below with the words in the box.

a bit of a waste of	ran out of
a bit short of	save
have you got	spent
make	worth

1a. They didn't tell me anything I didn't know already, so the meeting was . . . . time.

1b. I saw it by chance and bought it on impulse, but I've never used it, so it was . . . . money.

2a. I . . . . about three hours on Saturday sorting out the house, so it's nice and tidy now.

2b. We've . . . . quite a lot of money doing up the house, so it looks really nice now.

3a. I can't afford to go out at the moment. I'm . . . . money.

3b. Perhaps you could read this at home and talk about it next time. We're . . . . time today.

4a. Don't try to persuade him. It's not . . . . the time and effort. He's the most stubborn person I know.

4b. I wouldn't bother getting a new one. It's not . . . . the money. Second-hand ones are just as good, and they're half the price.

5a. I've started walking to school instead of taking the bus. I'm trying to . . . . money.

5b. Why do we have to fill in so many forms? If they just had one, it would . . . . everybody so much time.

6a. I didn't do all the questions in the exam because I . . . . time.

6b. I didn't spend as much time as I wanted in London because I . . . . money and had to come home.

7a. He's been really busy, but he's promised to .... time to do it next week.

7b. The business was slow to start with, but this year it has really taken off and we're hoping to .... a large profit.

8a. .... time for a cup of coffee, or do you need to rush back home?

8b. .... any money I could borrow? I've left my wallet in the office.

7 | Problems in shops

Make sentences describing things that can go wrong when you go shopping. Match the beginnings 1–4 to the endings a–d.

1. They didn't have the one I wanted in the first shop I went to, ☐

2. They didn't have any blue ones, ☐

3. They didn't accept credit cards, ☐

4. They didn't have any five-pound notes, ☐

a. so I bought a red one instead.

b. so I had to go to somewhere else instead.

c. so they had to give me it all in coins.

d. so I had to pay in cash.

Now make sentences by matching the beginnings 5–8 to the endings e–h.

5. I didn't have enough money for everything, ☐

6. I bought the wrong thing by mistake, ☐

7. They didn't have a very wide choice, ☐

8. They only had them in packs of six, ☐

e. and I didn't think you wanted that much, so I left it.

f. so I had to take it back and change it.

g. so I had to put some stuff back on the shelves.

h. so I just left it.

8 | Things we say in shops

Make sentences that customers often say by putting the words into the correct order.

1. Could / me / that / you / please / wrap / for / ?

....

2. I / take / please / Could / those / two / of / ?

....

3. I / think / leave / thanks / now / I'll / it / for

....

4. might / later / I / for / come / back / it

....

5. delivered / it / Could / get / I / ?

....

6. larger / got / a / you / in / Have / size / it / ?

....

7. it / Have / any / colours / got / other / you / in / ?

....

8. try / somewhere / Can / this / I / on / ?

....

9 | Supposed to

Choose the correct verb form.

1. It says in the contract *we're supposed to / we're not supposed to* put any pictures up on the walls, ☐

2. The doctor said *I'm supposed to / I'm not supposed to* try and bend my arm about forty times a day, ☐

3. I know *we're supposed / we're not supposed to* surf the Net at work, ☐

4. I know *we're supposed to / we're not supposed to* leave the office before five, ☐

5. Don't forget *we're supposed to / we're not supposed to* be meeting your parents for dinner tomorrow night, ☐

6. Don't forget *you're supposed to / you're not supposed to* know about Ray's surprise party, ☐

7. It says in the contract *we're supposed to / we're not supposed to* pay the rent on the last day of the month, ☐

8. The doctor said *I'm supposed to / I'm not supposed to* put any weight on my ankle for a few days, ☐

Now match the follow-up comments to 1–8 above.

a. but no one will notice if I sneak out five minutes early, will they?

b. so make sure you don't open your big mouth and tell him by accident!

c. so I was wondering if you could maybe pop out to the shops for me later?

d. but I'm sure it won't matter if it's a couple of days late.

e. but it's too painful to try at the moment.

f. but no one will notice if I just have a quick look at this website, will they?

g. but I can't imagine the landlord will mind if I just have a couple of posters here.

h. so make sure you don't arrange anything else for then, OK?

7 Complaints

1 Things we say in hotels

Complete these sentences by putting the words in brackets into the right order.

1. When do you . . . . ?
   (meals / serving / evening / stop)

2. Have you got any . . . . ?
   (three / rooms / double / nights / for)

3. Is there somewhere . . . . ?
   (these / safe / could / leave / I)

4. Is there somewhere . . . . ?
   (overnight / car / can / park / I / my)

5. Is it possible to have . . . . ?
   (our / breakfast / please / rooms / in)

6. Is it possible to . . . . ?
   (an / room / my / international / make / call / from)

7. Is it possible to . . . . ?
   (ironed / these / and / get / washed)

8. Do you think you could . . . . ?
   (please / into / taxi / me / town / a / order)

9. Can I . . . . ?
   (a / six / call / for / get / please / wake-up / thirty)

2 Problems in restaurants

Are the following said by:
a. **a customer to another customer?**
b. **a customer to a waiter?**
c. **a waiter to a customer?**

1. I'm sorry, but this is still cold in the middle. Can you heat it up properly?

2. I'm sorry, but I can't eat this. It's burnt. Can you bring me another one?

3. I'm sorry. That was so clumsy of me. I'll ask them for a cloth.

4. I'm sorry, but we actually booked the table for nine and it's already half past.

5. I'm sorry, but if you don't like it, you know where the door is.

6. I'm sorry, but I asked for the vegetarian option, not beef stew.

7. I'm sorry, but we only take cash or cheques.

8. I'm sorry. I don't know what happened. I'll ask them for a dustpan and brush. I'll order you another one.

Now complete the sentences below to report what happened in 1–8. Use the words in the box.

accept	mixed up	rude
caught	overbooked	spilt
knocked over	overcooked	undercooked
leave		

9. I had to send my main course back because it was . . . .

10. I had to ask them to re-do my starter because it was . . . .

11. It was a bit embarrassing. I . . . . my glass and . . . . wine all over the table.

12. We had to wait for ages because they'd . . . . the restaurant.

13. I couldn't believe it. The waiter was so . . . . ! He more or less told me to . . . . !

14. We had to wait for ages because they completely . . . . our order.

15. It was really embarrassing. I had to ask her to pay because they didn't . . . . credit cards.

16. It was really embarrassing. I must've . . . . the table as I went past and sent her plate flying.

3 Not very good

Complete these short dialogues by making polite negative sentences using the ideas in brackets. The first one is done for you:

1. A: Do you think this milk is OK?

   B: I'm not sure . *It doesn't smell very nice* , does it?
   (smell / nice)

2. A: Have you heard about Matthew? He didn't get into the university he applied to.

   B: Oh, really? I saw him earlier today and he . . . . , so that's probably why.
   (look / happy)

3. A: Do you think this sauce will be OK with the pudding?

   B: One minute … um … Haven't you added any sugar yet? It . . . . (taste / sweet)

4. A: Are you OK? You look a bit pale.

   B: Yeah, I know. I . . . . today. (feel / well)

5. A: What's that new cafe round the corner like? Have you tried it yet?

   B: No, but it . . . . , from what everyone's been saying. (sound / good)

6. A: I thought we ordered dry white wine. Try it. What do you think?

   B:. No, you're right. It . . . . , does it? Shall we ask the waiter to change it? (taste / dry)

7. A: Where were you yesterday? You missed a really funny lesson.

   B: Oh, I just . . . . , that's all. (feel / well)

8. A: Put your shoes back on! Your feet smell dreadful!

   B: Yeah, sorry. They . . . . , do they? (smell / nice)

9. A: Jack said his new flatmate is a bit of an idiot.

   B: I know. He told me too. He . . . . , does he? (sound / nice)

10. A: Shall we stay up and watch that thing that's on later?

    B: No, let's just leave it. It . . . . , judging from the advert they showed earlier. (look / interesting)

4 Commenting on what people say

Complete the short dialogues below with the comments in the box.

That's a shame	That's hilarious
That's awful	That's really annoying
That's brilliant	That's ridiculous
That's disgusting	

1. A: I had to complain to Reception, because I could see the sheets on the bed had been used before. They hadn't even washed or changed them!

   B: . . . . ! So, what did they do about it?

2. A: My grandmother died last night.

   B: . . . . ! I'm really sorry. Was it very sudden?

3. A: Listen, I'm sorry. I won't be able to come round for dinner after all.

   B: . . . . ! I was looking forward to it. Can you make it next week?

4. A: Someone switched off the computer by mistake and I lost what I was working on.

   B: . . . . ! Was it a lot of stuff?

5. A: They won't give me a work permit without a job, and I can't get a job without a permit.

   B: . . . . ! So, what are you going to do?

6. A: Anyway, his boss comes in and he's standing there with a paper bag over his head!

   B: . . . . ! So, what did he say?

7. A: I've got that job I applied for.

   B: . . . . ! So, when do you start?

5 Had to, didn't have to

Choose the correct form.

1. In our old flat, *we had to / we didn't have to* pay any of the bills. They were all included in the rent.

2. In our old flat, *we had to / we didn't have to* pay the rent weekly, not monthly.

3. In my old job, *I had to / I didn't have to* wear a suit and tie. I used to spend a fortune on clothes.

4. In my old job, *I had to / I didn't have to* start work until midday, so I got a lie-in every day.

5. It was horrible going to England because *I had to / I didn't have to* apply for a visa and it took ages.

6. It was simple going to Turkey because *we had to / we didn't have to* get a visa till we got there.

7. There was nothing wrong with it if you ask me. I don't know why *we had to / we didn't have to* get rid of it.

8. It was in a terrible state. I can't believe the council told them *they had to / they didn't have to* get rid of it.

6 Excuses

Complete these sentences by putting one of the verbs in brackets in the past simple (e.g., *went*) and using one of the verbs with *had to* (e.g., *had to go*).

1. A: Why didn't you call me last night?

   B: I . . . . my mum first, and by the time we . . . . talking, I thought it was a bit late to phone. (call, finish)

2. A: Why didn't you ring me back?

   B: Sorry, I . . . . to get something from the shops, and by the time I . . . . , I had forgotten. (pop out, get back)

3. A: Why didn't you come to the party last night?

   B: I was going to, but I suddenly . . . . I had a test this morning, so I . . . . and study. (remember, stay in)

4. A: Why didn't you come to the party last night?

    B: I was going to, but my parents . . . . to go out and I . . . . and look after my younger brother. (decide, stay in)

5. A: How come you were so late this morning?

    B: There . . . . a problem on the trains, and I . . . . on the platform for almost an hour. (be, wait)

6. A: How come you were so late this morning?

    B: I got halfway here and I . . . . I'd left my wallet at home, so I . . . . and get it. (realise, go back)

7. A: Why didn't you do your homework?

    B: I . . . . my mum to hospital, because she . . . . an accident while she was cooking. (take, have)

8. A: Why didn't you do your homework?

    B: I . . . . just very busy yesterday and I . . . . late, so I didn't have time. (be, work)

7 | It really gets on my nerves!

Complete the complaints below with the pairs of words in the box.

drives / anti-social	racist / black
hate / ruins	smoke / killing
moan / avoid	spit / disgusting

1. I can't stand people who . . . . in the street. It's . . . . !

2. I can't understand people who . . . . Don't they realise it's just a slow way of . . . . yourself?

3. I'm sick and tired of people who . . . . about the state of the health service, but who then . . . . paying taxes!

4. It . . . . me mad when people play really loud music on their car stereos. It's so . . . .

5. I get really upset with people making . . . . comments in front of me, especially because my wife is . . . .

6. I . . . . it when people forget to turn their mobile phones off in cinemas. It . . . . the film for everyone.

8 | More problems

Match the sentences 1–9 to the pictures A–H.

1. There's a crack in it. ☐
2. There's a tear in the sleeve. ☐
3. There's a stain on the front. ☐
4. There's a dent in the side. ☐
5. It's chipped on the edge here. ☐
6. The picture's fuzzy. ☐
7. The button's come off. ☐
8. The cover's damaged. ☐

A

B

C

D

E

Dicti

F

G

H

9 | Writing: a letter of complaint

Complete the letter of complaint below with the words in the box.

board	polite
compensation	possible
complain	refund
delayed	treated
explanation	upset

Dear Sir/Madam,

I am writing to (1) . . . . about my recent experiences with your airline and to ask you to consider suitable (2) . . . .

On October 25th 2002, I flew with your company from London Heathrow to Prague, and returned to London three days later. On the outbound flight, the plane was (3) . . . . for over four hours for some unspecified reason. When we were finally allowed to (4) . . . . the plane, no apology was made and no (5) . . . . was offered. Secondly, your flight attendants were not very (6) . . . . and the in-flight meals were almost cold by the time we were served them.

On the return flight, I wanted to bring some pottery I had bought in Prague as hand luggage, but was told this would not be (7) . . . . However, I was reassured that the package would be (8) . . . . with care, and so I agreed to check my goods in. You can imagine how (9) . . . . I was when I collected my package at London, only to find that the pottery had been smashed into little pieces. I complained to representatives of your company at the airport, but was told there was nothing that could be done.

I am naturally very unhappy about this state of affairs, and would like you to (10) . . . . me the full cost of my goods. Please find enclosed my receipt for the goods.

I look forward to hearing from you soon.

Yours faithfully,

Simon Kleinsmede

10 | Using the passive

In formal letters of complaint, it is quite common to use passive verb forms instead of active ones. They make our complaint sound less specific, and allow us to make general points without blaming specific people. The important thing we want to make clear is what happened, *not* who made it happen. Can you find the eleven examples of the passive in the letter in Exercise 9?

Make passive sentences from letters of complaint by matching the beginnings 1–8 to the endings a–h.

1. My luggage was ☐
2. The room had not been ☐
3. I was promised that ☐
4. I was told to ☐
5. The work was not ☐
6. The letter was ☐
7. I should have been ☐
8. Our booking should've been ☐

a. there would be a maximum of sixteen students per class, but this was untrue.

b. completed in time.

c. sent to me over three months ago, but I still haven't received it.

d. paid on the thirtieth of last month, but have yet to receive my wages.

e. cleaned.

f. confirmed in writing, but it never was.

g. lost somewhere between Moscow and Beijing.

h. report it to the customer care line, but when I tried to, the line was busy.

Now write your own letter of complaint about the following. Try to use some of the passive structures above. Can you find any more expressions from the letter in Exercise 9 which you think will help you?

You booked two tickets for a play last week over the phone. The person you spoke to told you they were going to send them to you, but they didn't. They did charge you for the tickets, though. You know, because you checked with your bank. You tried to phone and complain, but the line was always busy. On the night of the play, you went to the theatre with your partner and tried to explain things, but the person there said they had no record of your booking. You had to buy two tickets in horrible seats. You are not happy about it!

8 House and home

1 Who do you live with?

Make sentences describing who people live with by matching the beginnings 1–6 to the endings a–f.

1. I live on
2. I share a house
3. I still live at
4. I live with
5. She lives in
6. I share a room

a. home with my parents.
b. an old people's home.
c. my own.
d. with six other people.
e. my girlfriend.
f. in a student hall of residence.

Now match the follow-up comments i–vi to the speakers in 1–6 above:

i. It's nice having someone to come home to every day after work, but she's got some really annoying habits!
ii. It's nice getting all my cooking and washing done for me, but I wish I had more privacy sometimes.
iii. It's nice having someone to talk to, but it's a bit cramped – and he snores as well!
iv. It's nice because I get my own space and I get time to myself, but I do get a bit lonely sometimes.
v. It's nice because there's always someone around to talk to, but it can get very messy and noisy sometimes.
vi. It's nice because she gets to meet lots of other people the same age as her – and she gets well looked after.

2 What's your flat like?

Complete the sentences below with the words in the box.

brand new	cramped	run-down
bright	dark	spacious
convenient	noisy	

1. It's very . . . . It's the biggest place I've ever lived in in my life!
2. It's a bit . . . . I think we're going to have to get rid of half of our furniture!
3. It's nice and . . . . We've got huge big windows, and it faces south, so we get a lot of sunlight.
4. It's quite . . . . It's right on the main road.
5. It's very . . . . It's only two or three minutes' walk from the shops and the station.
6. It's a bit . . . . It's a basement flat, so we don't get much sunlight.
7. It's very . . . . We're going to have to spend a fortune doing everything up.
8. It's . . . . We've got a shiny new kitchen, a lovely new bathroom – it's great!

Which of the sentences above are negative?

3 Was it very expensive?

Match the topics 1–9 to the comments made about them a–i.

1. a car hire
2. a taxi ride
3. a self-catering holiday
4. your rent
5. a meal out
6. a hotel
7. a dishwasher
8. a suit
9. a motorbike

a. It wasn't too bad. It cost us twenty pounds each for three courses including wine.
b. No, it was really cheap, actually. It cost us twenty dollars a night including breakfast.
c. It wasn't too bad. It cost us just over 300 euros for ten days plus the petrol we used.
d. Yeah, it was terrible! It cost me eight hundred a month, and that was excluding bills!
e. Yeah, it was a rip-off! It cost me $50, and then he charged me another $5 just for putting my bags in the boot!
f. No, it was a bargain! It only cost $100 – reduced from $150 – and they gave me a free tie to go with it.
g. Yeah, it was a rip-off. It cost us a thousand for the week, and the whole place was really dark and cramped.
h. Yeah, it was a rip-off. It cost me five thousand, and then it broke down the first time I went out on it!
i. No, it was a bargain. It cost me $100 ten years ago and it's never broken down, and it still cleans everything perfectly.

4   Describing trends

Look at the graphs below and then complete the sentences by putting the verbs in the box into the right form. The first one is done for you.

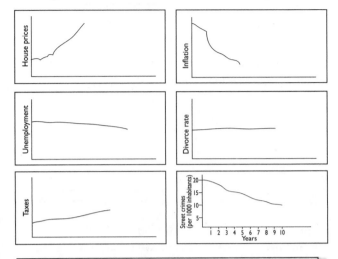

| fall dramatically | halve | rocket |
| fall slightly | rise slightly | stay fairly steady |

1. House prices *have rocketed* . . . over the last ten years.

2. Inflation . . . . over the last ten years.

3. Unemployment . . . . over the last ten years.

4. The divorce rate . . . . over the last ten years.

5. Taxes . . . . over the last ten years.

6. Street crime . . . . over the last ten years.

Are any of the sentences above true for your country?

5   Describing areas 1

Complete the four different descriptions below with the words in the boxes.

| afford | lift | own |
| city centre | nowhere | |

1. It's all right, but it's a bit boring. I mean, there's not really much to do at night. And the other thing is, we live in the middle of (a) . . . . There's only one bus into the (b) . . . . , and it only runs about once every hour. I have to rely on my parents giving me a(n) (c) . . . . if I want to go out to the cinema, which can be a real pain. Basically, it's the only place my parents could (d) . . . . to buy a house, and I do have my (e) . . . . room, which is good. Some of my friends at school have to share. When I was younger, I used to play in the garden quite a lot as well.

| balcony | noisy | tiny |
| everywhere | pain | |

2. It's a really nice place, but I'm not sure I'd want to live there. I mean, it's incredibly central. He's got a(n) (a) . . . . that overlooks Cavendish Square and he can basically walk (b) . . . . , but the flat's so small. It really is (c) . . . . and he has to pay something ridiculous like four hundred pounds a week. I don't know how he affords it. It must get quite (d) . . . . at night with all the bars and everything round there. I mean, that's OK if you want to go out, but if you want to have just a quiet night in, you can't get away from it, which must be a bit of a(n) (e) . . . .

| cheap | fix | share |
| cut off | rough | useless |

3. It's a bit (a) . . . . round there, to be honest. There's quite a lot of crime and graffiti, although I've never had any problems myself since I've been living there. One good thing is that it's incredibly (b) . . . . I only pay thirty pounds a week for a huge room in a house, which I (c) . . . . with five other students. We generally get on really well and we've had quite a few house parties, but we do sometimes argue about who's going to do the washing up and cleaning and how we pay the bills. Last month we had the phone (d) . . . . because we didn't pay the bill in time. The other thing is the landlord's (e) . . . . Last winter the central heating broke down, and it took him three weeks to get someone in to (f) . . . . it.

| dead | get away | privacy |
| fresh air | gossiping | right out |

4. I live (a) . . . . in the country in a little village. I hate it. I'm going to university next year and I can't wait to (b) . . . . I mean, the countryside is really nice and you've got (c) . . . . and all that, but at night it's just (d) . . . . Even the nearest video shop is five miles away. As for a club or anything like that, forget it! The other thing is there's just no (e) . . . . Everyone knows everyone else and they're always (f) . . . . and sticking their noses into your business.

6 Describing areas 2

Match the descriptions 1–8 to the comments a–h.

1. It's very convenient for the shops. ☐
2. It's dead at night. ☐
3. It's quite rough. ☐
4. It's very green. ☐
5. It's quite a posh area. ☐
6. It's very lively. ☐
7. It's quite dirty. ☐
8. It's really noisy. ☐

a. The other day, somebody got stabbed just round the corner from my flat.

b. The other day, I saw a gold Rolls Royce pull up outside a house over the road from my flat.

c. The other day, I came out of my house and somebody had dumped their rubbish in the street.

d. The other day, I was coming home quite late at night and the Greek supermarket over the road was still open!

e. I just couldn't get to sleep the other night because of all the traffic on the main road outside my flat.

f. I wanted to buy some milk the other evening, but I couldn't find anywhere open at all!

g. I found another nice park the other day near my son's school, so we went for a good long walk round there.

h. I found another great little restaurant the other day round the corner from those bars I was telling you about.

7 Describing people's bad habits

Complete the short dialogues below with the negative adjectives in the box.

boring	dishonest	mean
childish	forgetful	rude
clumsy	immature	unhealthy

1. A: He's always breaking in to conversations and demanding something or other!
   B: He sounds really . . . . if you ask me!

2. A: She's always eating junk food and chocolate and that kind of thing.
   B: Oh, really? She sounds quite . . . . to me.

3. A: He's always knocking things over and dropping things.
   B: Yeah? He sounds really . . . .

4. A: She's always sulking and getting angry and screaming and shouting!
   B: Oh, really? She sounds quite . . . . and . . . . to me.

5. A: He never tells the truth or lets me know where he's going.
   B: Oh, no! He sounds quite . . . . if you ask me.

6. A: She never shares anything or lets you borrow any of her things!
   B: Oh, no! She sounds really . . . .

7. A: He never remembers where he's put things!
   B: Oh, really? He sounds very . . . .

8. A: She never stops talking about her job and her boyfriend and her car!
   B: Oh, no! She sounds really . . . .

Language note

Did you notice that all of the responses in Exercise 7 use *He/She sounds ...*? If we've never met somebody, but we have an idea of what kind of person they are from what somebody tells us, we usually use *He/She sounds + adjective* to say what we think about them. We also often use this structure to talk about places, films, restaurants, etc. that we've heard about, but don't have any real experience of. For example:

I've never been to Hong Kong, but it sounds amazing, from what I've heard.

I haven't seen that film yet, but it doesn't really sound like my kind of thing. Everybody says it's quite violent.

8 Housework

Match the verbs 1–8 to the words they collocate with a–h.

1. hang out ☐
2. make ☐
3. water ☐
4. empty ☐
5. hoover ☐
6. clear ☐
7. sweep ☐
8. do ☐

a. the plants
b. the front room
c. the table after dinner
d. the washing
e. the patio
f. the dishwasher
g. the ironing
h. the beds

Now use some of the collocations to complete these sentences.

9. Do you think you could get me the broom from the cupboard under the stairs, please? I just want to . . . .

10. Do you think you could get me some pegs from the drawer in the kitchen? I just want to . . . .

11. Do you think you could get me the watering can? I just want to . . . . in the front garden.

12. Do you think you could set the board up there? I just want to . . . . quickly.

13. Do you think you could plug this in for me there, please? I just want to . . . .

14. Do you think you could . . . . for me, please, so I can get the washing-up done?

9 Collocations with *home* or *house*

Complete these sentences with *house(s)* or *home*.

1. Come in. Let me take your bags. Come and sit down. Make yourself at . . . .

2. I was brought up in a little village, but I left . . . . when I was sixteen and moved to the city.

3. Now we've had the baby, we need to move . . . . It's a bit cramped here with three of us.

4. The . . . . is quite run-down, but we're going to do it up ourselves.

5. The . . . . is in such a mess I'm going to have to do some tidying up tonight.

6. My gran's over eighty now and she lives in an old-people's . . . .

7. My mum's always complaining that my dad never does any of the . . . . work.

8. Our teacher's always giving us lots of . . . . work, but I never do any of it!

9. He comes from a broken . . . . His parents are divorced and his dad's an alcoholic.

10. I'm sick of sharing a . . . . The landlord's useless, and so are the people I live with!

11. My parents are going away, so we'll have the whole . . . . to ourselves for a few days.

12. I'd love to buy my own . . . . , but I can't afford it because . . . . prices are so high at the moment.

13. I usually have to work late, and even then I often have to take work . . . . with me.

14. They're going to knock down all those derelict . . . . and build a multiplex cinema.

10 Asking for permission and making requests

Complete these questions with *Is it OK if I* or *Do you think you could*.

1. . . . . just give me a hand with this if you don't mind? ☐

2. . . . . turn up a bit late tomorrow? I've got to take a friend of mine to the airport at eight. ☐

3. . . . . lend me your book for tonight? I've lost mine somewhere. ☐

4. . . . . borrow your car for an hour? I just want to pick something up. ☐

5. . . . . draw the curtains a bit? The sun's really getting in my eyes. ☐

6. . . . . give me a hand on Saturday? I'm moving house. ☐

7. . . . . borrow your mobile for a second? I just need to phone my mum. ☐

8. . . . . just help me sort the tables out for the class today? ☐

Now match the questions 1–8 above to the answers a–h.

a. Yeah, sure, no problem. How do you want them arranged? As normal?

b. Oh, sorry, but I'm already doing something else this weekend. Have you tried asking Albert?

c. Yeah, sure. It looks really heavy. Do you want me to see if I can find someone else to help as well?

d. Yeah, sure. Sorry. It is a bit bright, isn't it?

e. Oh, sorry, but I think I'm going to need it tonight. You could try asking Stephanie, maybe.

f. Yeah, of course, but make sure you're not too late.

g. Yeah, of course. Wait a minute. You're not insured, are you?

h. Yeah, of course. Go ahead. You'll have to press the 'on' button first, yeah?

> **Language note**
>
> When we ask other people for permission or make requests, it's normal to add a follow-up comment, explaining why we're asking. Did you notice the extra comments in questions 1–8 in Exercise 10? If you were asking the questions in your own language, would you add these kinds of follow-up comments?

1 Your computer

Label the picture of the computer below with the words in the box.

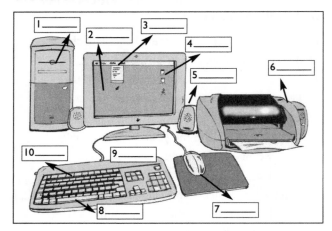

disk drive	keyboard	screen
file menu	mouse	space bar
F-keys	printer	speaker
icon		

Now complete these sentences with some of the words from the box above.

1. All you need to do to set up the program is load the disc and double-click on the . . . . that appears on the screen.

2. If you want to change the page size, bring up the . . . . and click on 'page set up'.

3. When's the last time you cleaned this . . . . ? The space bar's not working properly! It's filthy!

4. This bloody computer! The . . . . has frozen again. I don't know why it keeps doing it.

5. The sound quality's great, isn't it? Did the . . . . come with the computer or did you buy them as an add-on?

6. Why are you using the mouse to cut and paste? It's much quicker if you use the . . . .

7. The . . . . 's got jammed with paper again. There must be something wrong with it.

Underline the collocations above and try to remember them.

2 Talking about computers

Complete the sentences with the words in the box.

back	Internet	online
disc	laptop	re-boot
e-mails	memory	system
file		

1. I'm just going to check my . . . .
2. I can't open this . . . .
3. I spend too much time surfing the . . . .
4. I can't eject this . . . .
5. Somebody hacked into their . . . .
6. Make sure you save your work regularly. Then . . . . it up before you go home.
7. If it crashes, just . . . . it.
8. I always book flights . . . .
9. It's a bit slow. Why don't you buy some more . . . . ?
10. I take my . . . . home with me every night.

Now complete these sentences with words from sentences 1–10 above.

11. I won't be long. I'm just going to . . . . my e-mails.
12. If you just . . . . that file there, I think you'll find what you're looking for.
13. My brother's a real computer nerd! He spends hours and hours just . . . . the Net!
14. This disc is stuck inside somehow. I can't work out how to . . . . it.
15. If you go . . . . , I can't use the phone!

3 What software do you use?

Make sentences by matching the beginnings 1–6 to the endings a–f.

1. I use Outlook Express® to send ☐
2. I use Powerpoint® to write and give ☐
3. I use Photoshop® to manage and play around ☐
4. I use Adobe Acrobat® to send large files ☐
5. I use Word® all the time to write documents ☐
6. I use Excel® to do spreadsheets and present ☐

a. and letters and things like that.
b. presentations.
c. the company's finances.
d. with my digital photos.
e. e-mails.
f. over the Internet.

Which programs do you use?

4 Computers love them or hate them?

Complete the text below with the words in the box.

banking	junk e-mails	send
book	keep in touch	the news
can't stand	look things up	
deleting	order	

My girlfriend is a big computer fan! She's just crazy about them. She says that they've made her life so much easier. She can (1) .... with her all her friends all over the world by e-mail; she can (2) .... on the Internet, (3) .... flights, order books and CDs, even keep up with (4) .... from other countries; she can word-process documents and (5) .... photos over the web; she does all her (6) .... online and it even reminds her of when to buy birthday presents and send cards!

I'm the complete opposite! I (7) .... computers! Every time I touch one, it crashes or the screen just freezes. I keep getting sent endless (8) .... and I can't keep up with the ones I do want to reply to (it doesn't help that I'm a one-fingered typist!); I keep (9) .... files by accident, and every time I try and surf the Net, I just get lost in Cyberspace! The one time I did try and (10) .... some flowers for my girlfriend online, something went wrong with the system and they sent her fifteen bunches of roses instead of one – and then charged me for *thirty*! Computers? Who needs them?

Who are you more similar to, the writer or his girlfriend? Why?

5 Have you ever ...?

Complete these questions by putting the verbs in brackets into the correct form.

1. Have you ever .... to Japan? (go) ☐

2. Have you ever .... really badly homesick? (feel) ☐

3. Have you ever .... Vietnamese food? (try) ☐

4. Have you ever .... any films by Almodovar? (see) ☐

5. Have you ever .... anything by The Counts? (hear) ☐

6. Have you ever .... in a fight? (be) ☐

7. Have you ever .... food poisoning? (have) ☐

8. Have you ever .... off your bike? (fall) ☐

Now match the questions 1–8 to the answers a–h.

a. Yeah, I have, actually. It was when I first left home, and I really missed my mum and dad.

b. Yeah, I have, actually. I got it a few years ago in Pakistan. It was horrible!

c. Yeah, I have, actually. Quite a few times. It's really spicy. You'd like it.

d. Yeah, I have, actually. A few years ago. This car cut in front of me and I came off!

e. No, never. What kind of music do they play?

f. No, never. I've never even heard of him!

g. No, never. I've always been good at keeping out of trouble!

h. No, never, but I'd love to one day. I've heard it's amazing.

6 Superlatives with the present perfect

We often use superlatives (e.g., *the best, the nicest, the most interesting*) with the present perfect and the words *in a long time* and *ever*. For example:

It was one of the best parties I've been to for a long time. It's a shame you couldn't come.

He's one of the nicest people I've ever met. He wouldn't hurt a fly.

Complete the short dialogues below with the correct form of the pairs of words in the box.

bad / have	funny / meet	posh / stay in
boring / meet	good / go to	

1. A: What was the restaurant like?
   B: Awful! It's the .... meal .... for a long time.

2. A: What was the concert like?
   B: Brilliant! It's one of the .... gigs .... ever ....

3. A: What was the hotel like?
   B: Amazing! It's probably the .... ever ....

4. A: What was her boyfriend like?
   B: Terrible! He was one of the .... men .... ever ....

5. A: What's Tim like?
   B: Oh, he's hilarious! Honestly, he's one of the .... people .... ever ....

Now complete the short dialogues below with the correct form of the pairs of words in the box.

bad / see	enjoyable / had	sad / heard
disgusting / see	good / read	

6. A: Did you have a good time last night?

    B: Yeah. It was the . . . . night out . . . . for a long time. Thanks for inviting me.

7. A: What did you think of the film?

    B: I think that's probably the . . . . film . . . . ever . . . . It was awful!

8. A: Have you ever read *The Autobiography of Malcolm X*?

    B: Yeah, it's brilliant! It's one of the . . . . books . . . . ever . . . .

9. A: Have you heard Michael's joined a dating agency?

    B: You're joking! That's the . . . . thing . . . . in a long time. He must be desperate.

10. A: Look, I can fit a whole chocolate bar in my mouth!

    B: Oh, no. I think that's the . . . . thing . . . . in a long time.

7   Replying to advice

Put the conversations below into the correct order.

Conversation 1

a. No, I hadn't thought of that. ☐

b. Have you tried getting some more memory put in? ☐

c. Well, try that. Otherwise, there's not much you can do. ☐

d. I'm sick of this computer. It's so slow, but I can't afford a new one. ☐

Conversation 2

a. Well, in that case, if I were you, I'd tell him you'll phone the police if he doesn't stop bothering you. ☐

b. Yeah, I tried that, but he didn't take the hint. ☐

c. Have you tried telling him you're not interested? ☐

d. This guy keeps phoning me up and asking me out. ☐

Conversation 3

a. Yeah, I tried that, but I didn't have much success. ☐

b. Oh, right. Well, in that case, I can't really help. ☐

c. I've been looking for this book I want to buy for ages, but I can't find it anywhere. ☐

d. If I were you, I'd try looking on the Internet. ☐

Conversation 4

a. Poor you! Has he tried cutting out coffee from his diet. It's supposed to help. ☐

b. I'm exhausted. John's been keeping me awake with his snoring. It's awful. ☐

c. Well, you should tell him to give it a go. Otherwise, I'd start sleeping in separate bedrooms if I were you. You look awful! ☐

d. No, I've never heard of that before. ☐

8   Responding to advice

Below are eight fixed phrases for responding to advice. Complete them with the words in the box.

do	hint	suggest
good	one	work
help	success	

1. I did that, but I didn't have much . . . .

2. I tried that, but he didn't take the . . . .

3. I tried that, but it didn't . . . .

4. I did that, but it didn't do any . . . .

5. Try that. Otherwise, there's not much you can . . . .

6. Try that. Otherwise, I can't really . . . .

7. Try that. Otherwise, I don't know what else to . . . .

8. Try that. Otherwise, you'll have to get a new . . . .

9   Keep + -ing

Complete the short dialogues below with the words in the box.

aggressive	forgetful	nosy
bossy	naughty	polite

1. A: He keeps locking himself out of the house and forgetting all kinds of things.

    B: I know. He can be very . . . . sometimes, can't he?

2. A: He keeps opening doors for me and making me coffee.

    B: I know. He's a bit too . . . . sometimes, isn't he?

3. A: He keeps getting in fights and picking on his younger brothers.

   B: I know. He can be a very . . . . child sometimes, can't he?

4. A: She keeps trying to tell me what to do and ordering me around.

   B: I know. She can be very . . . . sometimes, can't she?

5. A: She keeps asking me all kinds of personal questions.

   B: I know. She can be very . . . . sometimes, can't she?

6. A: She keeps throwing her toys around and answering back!

   B: I know. She can be a very . . . . child sometimes, can't she?

10 Collocations with *mistake*

Complete the sentences below with the words in the box.

admit	expensive	makes
biggest	learn from	spelling
discover	made	took

1. Look at this letter. It's full of . . . . mistakes. They should've used the spell checker!

2. Everybody . . . . mistakes. The important thing is to make sure you . . . . them.

3. Sorry, I think this is your book. I . . . . it home by mistake last lesson.

4. The bank added $500 to my account last year. They didn't . . . . their mistake until I'd spent it all!

5. I . . . . the mistake of talking to Judith yesterday. Honestly, I was there for hours. I was late for my meeting.

6. It was quite a(n) . . . . mistake. I think the company lost fifty thousand pounds because of it.

7. Honestly, if they get married, it'll be the . . . . mistake of their lives.

8. I wish he'd just . . . . he's made a mistake, but he's still insisting he's right.

Now go back and underline the collocations with *mistake*.

Learning tip

Lots of the most common nouns in English are 'empty nouns'. They mean different things in different contexts, depending on what they refer to. Words like *mistake*, *problem*, *situation*, *question*, *answer* and so on, have lots and lots of collocations. It's a good idea to try and keep a record of the collocations you meet for each of these words. Maybe you could keep a page for each word in your vocabulary notebook.

11 Writing: e-mails

Make sentences that we often use when beginning e-mails by matching 1–6 to a–f.

1. Just a quick e-mail to let you ☐
2. Just a quick one to say sorry ☐
3. Just a quick e-mail to say thank you for ☐
4. Just a quick one to remind you ☐
5. Just a quick e-mail to say ☐
6. Just a quick one to ask you ☐

a. putting me up over the weekend.
b. I couldn't make it to the party the other day.
c. if you're free next Thursday evening.
d. I got back home safely and am fine.
e. know I've arranged the meeting for Friday at seven thirty.
f. it's Mum's birthday next Monday.

Complete the short e-mail below with the words in the box.

add	last
arranged	look forward to
e-mail	

JUST A QUICK E-MAIL TO LET YOU KNOW I'VE (7) . . . . THE MEETING FOR FRIDAY AT SEVEN THIRTY. IT'S GOING TO BE IN ROOM 251 AND SHOULD ONLY (8) . . . . AN HOUR OR SO. IF THERE'S ANYTHING YOU WANT TO (9) . . . . TO THE AGENDA, COULD YOU (10) . . . . ME BY WEDNESDAY AT THE LATEST? (11) . . . . SEEING YOU THEN,

KEN

Now write five other short e-mails beginning with the sentences 2–6 in Exercise 11. Each e-mail should be under 75 words.

10 Meeting people

1 Sorry I'm late

Make excuses for being late by matching the beginnings 1–10 to the endings a–j.

1. The traffic on the main road ☐
2. There was a problem on ☐
3. I had to wait ages ☐
4. I forgot my mobile phone ☐
5. I had a bit of a problem ☐
6. I had to work a bit ☐
7. It took me longer to get here ☐
8. It just took me ages ☐
9. It took me ages to find ☐
10. My bicycle got ☐

a. getting my car started.
b. and had to go back home to get it.
c. to get myself ready.
d. later than I was expecting.
e. than I was expecting.
f. somewhere to park.
g. the underground.
h. a puncture.
i. was awful!
j. for the bus.

2 Keyword: *main*

Complete the sentences below with the words in the box.

course	meal	thing
difference	reason	tourist area
entrance	road	
line	square	

1. I live on a main . . . . , so it's really noisy at night. The traffic is crazy sometimes!

2. It's the first day I've really had the chance to get away from the main . . . . and actually explore the city.

3. I'll meet you at the university, outside the main . . . . Not that side door, but the big wooden ones, OK?

4. A: It's not the most interesting job in the world, but it is well-paid, and at least I know it's secure.
   B: Well, that's the main . . . . , isn't it?

5. The main . . . . between Latvia and Lithuania is that there are a lot more Russians living in Latvia.

6. It's on the main London to Brighton . . . ., so there should be plenty of trains there.

7. I think I'm going to have the soup as a starter, and then I'm not sure about the main . . . . yet.

8. A: So why did you two stop being friends, then?
   B: It's a long story, but I think the main . . . . is that as we got older, we just grew apart, really.

9. I usually work really late, so I try to have a large lunch and make that my main . . . . of the day.

10. I'll meet you at about nine, in the main . . . ., next to the fountain and that statue of Byron.

3 Using the infinitive to express purpose

We often explain why we do something by using an infinitive instead of *because* or *so*. For example:

I'm having a party because it's my birthday and I'm celebrating. = I'm having a party to celebrate my birthday.

Match the actions 1–10 to the actions a–j.

1. I'm going to the internet café ☐
2. I'm meeting up with a big group of friends tonight ☐
3. I often meet up with some friends in the park ☐
4. I'm just going to the bank ☐
5. I'm just popping out to the shops ☐
6. I'm going into town ☐
7. I'm going round to a friend's house this evening ☐
8. I'm going to Munich ☐
9. I've decided to move back in with my parents ☐
10. I'm taking a year out before I start work ☐

a. to play football.
b. to pay this cheque in.
c. to visit a friend who lives there.
d. to go clubbing.
e. to buy something to wear for a wedding.
f. to go travelling.
g. to play cards.
h. to save some money.
i. to get some milk.
j. to send an e-mail.

Learning tip

You could test yourself by covering a–j and trying to remember the endings. Another thing you could do is try to think of a different ending in each case. Use a dictionary when you don't know the word.

4 A night out

Complete the tables of collocations using the following words:

interval	seat	table
popcorn	stalls	tickets
portions	standing ovation	tip
programme	starter	trailers
row	subtitles	waiter

Restaurant

book a(n) . . . .
catch the . . . . 's eye
have a(n) . . . .
leave the waiter a(n) . . . .
they serve big . . . .

Cinema

book . . . .
sit in the back . . . .
eat some . . . .
watch the . . . . before the film
the film has . . . .

Theatre

book a(n) . . . .
sit in the . . . .
buy a(n) . . . .
have a(n) . . . . of fifteen minutes
give the actors a(n) . . . .

Learning tip

Cover the tables and see if you can remember the collocations that go with each word in the list.

5 Arranging to meet

Complete this phone conversation with the expressions in the box.

arranged	let you know	was wondering if
get ready	on the safe side	where I mean
I'm wrong	the plan	

Stella: Hello.

Martin: Oh, hi, Stella. It's me, Martin.

Stella: Oh, hi. How're things?

Martin: Yeah, good. Listen, I'm just phoning to (1) . . . . what's going on tonight.

Stella: Oh, OK. Great. So what's (2) . . . . ?

Martin: Well, I've (3) . . . . to go bowling in Moortown with Jamie and Rachel, and I (4) . . . . you and Mike would like to join us?

Stella: Yeah, that'd be great. What time are you meeting?

Martin: I think we said eight, but let's say ten to, just to be (5) . . . .

Stella: Yeah, OK. That sounds great. That'll give Mike plenty of time to (6) . . . . after he gets home from work.

Martin: OK. Do you know the bowling place there?

Stella: Yeah, I think so, but could you tell me again, just in case (7) . . . .

Martin: Yeah, sure. It's on the Otley Road, just near Moortown Station. Do you know (8) . . . . ?

Stella: Yeah, it's the place I was thinking of.

Martin: OK. Well, we're meeting there, just inside the entrance, in the foyer.

Stella: OK. Great. We'll see you there, then.

Martin: Yeah, OK. Bye.

Stella: Bye.

6 I'm just phoning to ...

Complete the short dialogues below with the pairs of words in the box.

cancelled / relief	meet up / I'm afraid
check / much better	OK for / forgotten
come over / what time	remember / reminding
house-warming party / moved	see / going away

1. A: I'm just phoning to see if you wanted to
    .... later.
    B: Oh, I'd love to, but .... I can't. I'm already doing something else.

2. A: I'm just phoning to see if you're still ....
    next Wednesday.
    B: Yeah, I know. Don't worry. I haven't .... It was seven o'clock, wasn't it?

3. A: I'm just phoning to .... what you're doing this weekend.
    B: Oh, I'm afraid we're .... for a few days this Friday. Why?

4. A: I'm just phoning to ask if you wanted to
    .... later for dinner.
    B: Yeah, that'd be great. .... would you like us to come?

5. A: I'm just phoning to invite you and Carol to our
    ....
    B: Oh, you've finally ...., have you? That's great. Yeah, we'd love to come.

6. A: I'm just phoning to let you know the meeting tomorrow has been ....
    B: Oh, OK. That's quite a ...., actually, because I'm really busy tomorrow! Thanks for telling me.

7. A: I'm just phoning to make sure you ....
    we're meeting Julian and Junko later.
    B: Oh, thanks for .... me. I'd completely forgotten about that.

8. A: I'm just phoning to .... how you are.
    B: Oh, I'm OK, thanks. I'm actually feeling ....
    today.

7 I'm not bothered

***Bother* is a very common word in English. We use it in a number of set phrases.**

don't bother	I wouldn't bother if I were you
I'm not bothered	it doesn't bother me
I can't be bothered	sorry to bother you
I don't bother	

Complete these sentences with one of the phrases in the box above.

1. A: Are you going to go to the meeting later?
    B: I should really, but .... I just can't face it. I'm too tired.

2. A: I was thinking of going to see that new Mike Leigh film tonight.
    B: Oh, yeah? .... I saw it at the weekend and I fell asleep halfway through. It's really boring.

3. A: .... , but I'm looking for a shop called Rosie's. Do you know it?
    B: Sorry, I'm not from round here myself. Why don't you ask one of the waiters? They might know.

4. A: Don't you get sick of teaching the same thing every term?
    B: No, ... Anyway, it's never exactly the same and the students are all different.

5. A: Shall we stop and have some lunch?
    B: Yeah, if you like. .... with it usually. I'm happy working through till four and leaving early.

6. A: Can I help you with anything? Do you want me to lay the table or something?
    B: No, it's OK. .... I'll do it. You just sit down and take it easy.

7. A: What do you want to do? Shall we phone for a takeaway or do you want to eat out?
    B: It's up to you. .... either way.

8 Adding extra comments

Complete the short dialogues 1–8 below with the comments a–h.

1. A: Do you fancy going swimming later?
   B: To be honest, I'd rather go for a run. ☐

2. A: Would you like to go to visit my parents this weekend?
   B: To be honest, I'd prefer to stay at home and catch up with work. ☐

3. A: Do you want to go to that concert next Friday?
   B: Yeah, that'd be great. Shall we phone now and book the tickets? ☐

4. A: Do you want to go to that club, Roxy's, tonight?
   B: To be honest, I'd rather go to Rock City instead. ☐

5. A: Do you fancy eating Chinese for dinner tonight?
   B: To be honest, I'd prefer to eat Mexican instead. ☐

6. A: Would you like to go to a cafe for lunch?
   B: Yeah, that'd be great. Shall we try that new place round the corner? ☐

7. A: Do you fancy going to the karaoke night tomorrow?
   B: Yeah, that'd be great. Shall we invite Katy as well? ☐

8. A: Do you want to come shopping with me on Saturday?
   B: Yeah, that'd be great! Would it be OK if my brother comes along as well? ☐

a. They might sell out otherwise.

b. I just feel like something nice and spicy and, anyway, I had noodles for lunch.

c. I've heard she's got a really good singing voice.

d. I was off sick last week and I've got hundreds of e-mails I need to answer.

e. It's too cold to go into the sea today.

f. He's staying at my place for the weekend.

g. They've got a special offer on because it's just opened – two meals for the price of one.

h. The music's just much better there. And it's cheaper for students on a Thursday.

9 Verb patterns

Complete the sentences below with the words in the box.

avoiding	insisted	persuade	warn
fancy	let	refusing	
get used to	offered	regret	

1. I've been trying to . . . . my dad to buy me a car for ages, but he's still . . . . to give in.

2. I . . . . to give him some money, but he . . . . on paying for everything, so it was a cheap night.

3. I've been . . . . doing this essay for history class for ages, but the deadline's tomorrow.

4. It took me ages to . . . . living here, and now I've got to move away. It's such a pain!

5. Shall we go for Mexican? I . . . . eating something hot and spicy.

6. I'll . . . . you see mine if I can see yours.

7. A: I really . . . . going now. It was such a waste of time. I should've just stayed at home.
   B: Well, I did . . . . you not to go, but you wouldn't listen, would you?

Did you notice the pattern that follows each of the verbs above? Put the verbs in brackets into the correct form. Look at the sentences above to help you if you need to.

8. I tried to persuade him . . . . (come), but he insisted on . . . . (stay) at home.

9. It's been difficult, but I'm slowly getting used to him not . . . . (be) there.

10. I really regret not . . . . (buy) shares in the BAG company. They'd be worth £50 each now.

11. I'd rather just stay in tonight. I don't fancy . . . . (have) another night with two hours' sleep.

12. I offered . . . . (pay) for the damage, but he's still refusing . . . . (talk) to me.

13. Did you see the weather forecast? They're warning people . . . . (avoid) . . . . (travel) by car because of the wind.

14. He never lets me . . . . (get) a word in. He just talks and talks and talks. It's so annoying!

10 Do you want to ... , or shall we ...?

Make questions by matching the beginnings 1–6 to the endings a–f.

1. Do you want to eat out, ☐
2. Do you want to meet at around five, ☐
3. Do you want to meet in the foyer, ☐
4. Do you want to go and see *Lovers* while it's still on, ☐
5. Do you want to go for a starter, ☐
6. Do you want to split the bill, ☐

a. or shall we just have a main course?

b. or shall we just pay separately?

c. or shall we make it later?

d. or shall I come up to your room?

e. or shall we save money and make something here?

f. or shall we just wait until it comes out on DVD?

1 Cars

Can you find these things in the picture?

back window	indicator
boot	mirror
door	tyre
engine	windscreen

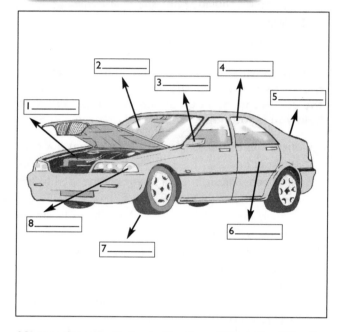

Now write words from the box above the list of collocations.

1. . . . .
   put your bags in the ... , I just want to make sure the ... 's locked properly

2. . . . .
   close the ... , that ... isn't closed properly, lock your ...

3. . . . .
   the ... need some air in them, one of the ... has got a puncture, check the spare ...

4. . . . .
   use your ... , the ... isn't working properly, your right ... , your left ...

5. . . . .
   the ... overheated, a very powerful ... , get the ... repaired, keep the ... running

6. . . . .
   I can't see out of the ... , Can you have a look out of the ... for me?, the ... is filthy

7. . . . .
   adjust the ... , look in the ... , clean the ... , a wing ... , the rear-view ...

8. . . . .
   clean the ... , scrape the ice off the ... , a stone shattered the ... , turn the ... wipers on

2 Tend to

When we are talking about things which usually – but don't always – happen, we often use *tend to* instead of an adverbial phrase. For example:

As a rule, I don't go to bed until quite late. (adverbial phrase)

I tend not to go to bed until quite late. (*tend to* + verb)

Re-write these sentences in a similar way to the example above.

1. We usually go out on a Friday.
   We . . . . out on a Friday.

2. As a rule, we don't go out during the week.
   We . . . . out during the week.

3. Generally speaking, I do the cooking and my wife does the washing-up.
   I . . . . the cooking and my wife . . . . the washing-up.

4. Generally speaking, British people are quite friendly.
   British people . . . . quite friendly.

5. People don't generally leave tips in my country.
   People . . . . tips in my country.

6. By and large, people are more generous in the north than in the south.
   People . . . . more generous in the north than in the south.

7. On the whole, the people there were very helpful.
   The people there . . . . very helpful.

8. On the whole, when I was working there, I didn't eat lunch.
   When I was working there, I . . . . lunch.

3 How did it happen?

Make sentences describing how different accidents happened by matching the beginnings 1–8 to the endings a–h.

1. This idiot went through ☐
2. This idiot was doing seventy ☐
3. This idiot was overtaking ☐
4. This idiot was driving ☐
5. This idiot cut ☐
6. This idiot was driving without ☐
7. It was very cold and we skidded ☐
8. I had to swerve to ☐

a. on a blind corner and crashed straight into them.
b. his headlights on and we didn't see him – until it was too late!
c. in front of us and we went straight into the back of him.
d. on some black ice.
e. avoid an old lady – and crashed straight into another car.
f. the red lights and crashed into the side of me.
g. too close to us and when we braked, he went into the back of us.
h. in a forty-kilometres-an-hour area.

Now see if you can complete the collocations 9–16 without looking at 1–8 above.

9. . . . . the red lights
10. overtake on a blind . . . .
11. swerve to . . . . a cat
12. . . . . on the ice
13. drive . . . . your headlights on
14. . . . . in front of us
15. crash into the . . . . of the car in front of me
16. . . . . ninety kilometres an hour

4 Comparing now with the past

Read the statement in the box. Circle the words which match. The first one is done for you.

> The country is much worse than it used to be.

1. It's *more* / *less* violent than it used to be.
2. People aren't as *rude* / *polite* as they used to be.
3. Unemployment is *higher* / *lower* than it used to be.
4. There's *more* / *less* crime than there used to be.
5. The cities aren't as *dirty* / *clean* as they used to be.

Now read the statement in the box. Circle the words which match. The first one is done for you.

> The country's much better than it used to be.

6. It isn't as *safe* / *dangerous* as it used to be.
7. Inflation is much *lower* / *higher* than it used to be.
8. It's *easier* / *more difficult* to find a job than it used to be.
9. They're finally spending *less* / *more* on health and education than they used to.
10. There aren't as many *policemen* / *drug addicts* on the street as there used to be.

How many of the sentences above describe your country?

5 Fixed comparative phrases

Make short dialogues by matching 1–6 to the responses with fixed comparative phrases a–f.

1. Sorry I'm late. I got held up at work. ☐
2. Which wine shall we get? ☐
3. Shall I give it to you tomorrow morning? ☐
4. Is this piece large enough for you? ☐
5. Do you mind if I come along with you later on? ☐
6. How much wood shall we get for the fire? ☐

a. Well, to be honest, the bigger, the better.
b. Yeah. The sooner, the better, really.
c. No, of course not. The more, the merrier.
d. The cheaper, the better. They all taste the same to me.
e. As much as you can carry. I don't want to run out later.
f. Never mind. Better late than never.

6 More comparatives

We do not just use adjectives to make comparisons. We also often make comparisons using adverbs when we want to compare the way something was done now with the way it was done in the past. We usually make comparisons using adverbs by adding -er for adverbs of one syllable and *more* before adverbs with two syllables. For example:

Can you say it a bit louder?
You should listen more carefully.

However, there are also some irregular forms. Complete these sentences with the comparative form of the adverbs in brackets, and see if you know the two irregular forms!

1. I finished the exam much .... than I thought I would. (quickly)

2. I used to go swimming .... than I do now. (often)

3. If you want to pass, you'll need to start checking your spelling much .... than you have been. (carefully)

4. This new car I've got runs much .... than the old one I had. (smoothly)

5. Anna works much .... than most of the rest of the people in her office. (hard)

6. He drives much .... (fast) than he should – and he knows it too!

7. Children write .... (badly) than twenty years ago and do .... (badly) at school.

8. Inter Milan played much .... last season. (well)

7 Nightmare journeys

Make sentences describing mistakes and their results by matching the beginnings 1–7 to the endings a–g.

1. I couldn't remember the number of the house, so I ended up going up ☐

2. We took the wrong turning and ended up going round ☐

3. I fell asleep on the train and ended up going miles past ☐

4. I took the northbound train instead the southbound one and ended up going miles in ☐

5. I got on the wrong bus by mistake and ended up in the middle ☐

6. I misheard the announcement at the airport and ended up waiting at ☐

7. He somehow managed to get on the wrong plane and ended up ☐

a. my stop!

b. and round in circles!

c. Gate 13 instead of Gate 30!

d. and down the street for ages!

e. in London instead of Rome!

f. of nowhere!

g. the wrong direction!

8 Collocations with *rough*

Complete the sentences below with the expressions in the box.

> a good night's sleep
> calmer
> know exactly
> much better
> smooth
> somewhere cleaner and safer
> somewhere with better discipline
> write it up more neatly

1. I had a really rough night last night because the baby woke me up three times. I hope I get .... tonight.

2. It was quite a rough area, so we decided to move to ....

3. I was feeling a bit rough this morning. I thought I was going to be sick, but I feel .... now.

4. If you want, write the letter in rough first and I'll have a look at it. You can then .... and send it.

5. When you try to stick the two pieces together, glue the rough sides and keep the .... sides facing outwards.

6. The ferry crossing was really rough. I got so sea-sick. I hope it's .... on the way back.

7. At a rough guess, I'd say it'll cost around £300 to repair, but I'll .... once I've had a proper look at it.

8. I went to a rough school where there was a lot of violence and bullying, so I'm going to send my kids ....

Go back and underline all the collocations with *rough*.

Learning tip

As you can see from Exercise 8, the idea of opposites is more difficult than many people think. What's the opposite of *rough*? Well, it depends. The opposite of *a rough area* is *a clean and safe area*, but the opposite of *a rough guess* is *knowing exactly*! This is why it's a bad idea to translate single words. It's always better to translate adjective + noun or verb + noun collocations instead.

9 What a stupid thing to do!

Make examples of the kinds of problems you might have when you're travelling by matching the beginnings 1–6 to the endings a–f.

1. I was caught speeding on the motorway. ☐
2. I was stopped for drink-driving. ☐
3. I was caught without a ticket. ☐
4. I was overweight on my baggage allowance. ☐
5. I got a parking ticket, ☐
6. I set off all the alarms going through security. ☐

a. because I was in a no-parking zone.
b. They let me take everything, but I had to pay a sixty-three-pound penalty.
c. I think it must've been because of my metal hip!
d. They gave me a breath test, but luckily, I was OK!
e. I had to pay the full return fare and a fifty-pound fine.
f. I was doing over a hundred, apparently. I couldn't believe it!

Which three people above were driving?

Which two were flying?

Which one was taking the train?

10 Writing: connecting ideas

Look at the underlined words we use to connect ideas within a sentence and between sentences. Notice how they are used. Can you translate them into your language?

a. In what part of the sentence do you find them?
b. What do you notice about the punctuation?
c. What kind of words go before/after them? Nouns? Pronouns and verb + -ing forms?

We forgot our passports, <u>so</u> we had to go back and get them. <u>Then</u> there was a big traffic jam on the way to the airport <u>because of</u> some road works, <u>so</u> we were even later. <u>By the time</u> we got there, there were no seats left on the plane. <u>Despite</u> our having tickets, the airline company wouldn't give us a seat on the plane. We tried to argue, <u>but</u> they wouldn't change their mind, <u>so</u> we had to wait three hours for the next one. The wait wasn't too bad, <u>though</u>, <u>because</u> I was reading this really good book.

Now complete the story below with the words in the box.

because	but	despite	then
because of	by the time	so	though

Hi Kolo,

Just a quick e-mail to say we finally got home safely and to say thanks for having us to stay. We haven't enjoyed ourselves so much for a long time. I have to say, the journey home was a bit of a nightmare, (1) . . . . It took us almost 25 hours in the end. (2) . . . . having your very clear instructions, we managed to get lost trying to get out of Paris and ended up driving towards Normandy instead of Calais. (3) . . . . we got back on the right road, we'd missed the ferry and had to wait for the next one. (4) . . . . we got caught in this awful storm, so we were delayed even more. In the end, we didn't leave Calais till two o'clock in the morning. We were all terribly sea-sick (5) . . . . the rough sea. I knew we should have got the Eurostar train. We got into Dover at around four o'clock, so there was hardly any traffic. (6) . . . . we were almost the only people on the motorway, we were racing along, when, would you believe it, we broke down! We called out the emergency breakdown service, but we had to wait almost an hour. When he got there, he decided he couldn't repair the car on the motorway, (7) . . . . he towed us the rest of the way to Orpington. As you can imagine, we were absolutely exhausted by the time we got home, (8) . . . . we both had to go straight into work that day. I was so tired I fell asleep in a meeting. It was quite embarrassing, I can tell you!

Anyway, thanks again for everything. I'll e-mail you again soon. I'm off to bed now.

Love,

Charlotte

Write your own e-mail starting in the same way, and explaining about the awful journey you had on the way to somewhere. Try and use as many of the connecting words from above as you can.

12 Food

1 It's a kind of …

Match the descriptions 1–8 to the pictures A–H.

1. It's a kind of board game.
2. It's a kind of game you play in winter.
3. It's a kind of fruit.
4. It's a kind of vehicle.
5. It's a kind of animal.
6. It's a kind of insect.
7. It's a kind of building.
8. It's a kind of drink.

 A

 B

 C

 D

 E

 F

 G

 H

Now match the follow-up comments i–viii to the descriptions 1–8 above.

i. It's a bit like a church.
ii. It's a bit like a pineapple, but bigger.
iii. It's a bit like bowling, except on ice.
iv. It's a bit like a kind of three-wheeled taxi.
v. It's a bit like whisky, but clear.
vi. It's a bit like chess, but with flat, round pieces.
vii. It's a bit like a small lion.
viii. It's a bit like a fly or something like that.

2 *Too* and *enough*

Complete these sentences with *too* or *enough*.

1. This soup is actually a bit . . . . spicy for me.
2. I don't think it's ready yet. It's not quite salty . . . .
3. Most English breakfasts that you get in cafes are just a bit . . . . greasy for my liking.
4. This is actually a bit . . . . sweet for me, to be honest.
5. Hey, don't eat any more or there won't be . . . . for everyone else.
6. I can't use this fish. It's not fresh . . . .
7. I don't think I've got . . . . money to pay the bill.
8. I can't decide where to eat tonight. There's just . . . . much choice in this town!

3 There's too much / There are too many

We use *there's too much* + uncountable nouns. For example:

There's too much sex and violence on TV.
There's too much salt in this soup.

We use *there are too many* + countable nouns. For example:

There are too many cars on the road.
There are too many little bones in some fish.

Complete these sentences with *there's too much* or *there are too many*.

1. I want to move. crime in our area.

2. I want to move. . . . . litter and rubbish on the streets round here.

3. They shouldn't let them build a new airport here. . . . . already . . . . planes going over my house.

4. They shouldn't let them build any more motorways. . . . . already . . . . noise and traffic.

5. They shouldn't let them build another golf course. already and they use up too much water.

6. The government wants to ban begging. They say . . . . beggars on the streets.

7. The government wants to ban cigarette advertising. They say there . . . . deaths from smoking.

8. They should ban Christmas. fun and happiness in the world, and it costs too much!

4 Keyword: *food*

Complete the sentences below with words in the box.

dog	health
fast	junk
foreign	left over
genetically-modified	organic

1. If there's any food . . . ., just put it in the fridge, and we can finish it off tomorrow.

2. If you see a pet shop later, remind me that I need to pop in and get some . . . . food.

3. It's no wonder he's obese! All he ever eats is . . . . food. I mean, he lives on burgers and french fries!

4. I don't like the idea of farmers using chemicals on the stuff they grow, so I buy a lot of . . . . food.

5. My grandmother only ever eats English food. I don't think she's ever tried . . . . food in her life!

6. We are running a bit late. There's a(n) . . . . food place round the corner if you want to grab something to eat.

7. I'm really worried about the way that big companies are trying to force everyone to start growing . . . . food.

8. She eats quite a lot of . . . . food – you know, beans, lentils, vegetables, fresh fruit, all that kind of thing.

Now match 9–16 to a–h.

9. It's no wonder you're getting fat. ☐
10. We'd better do some shopping later on today. ☐
11. If you do decide to have a party, let me know ☐
12. Make sure you wash you hands properly ☐
13. I've got to try and lose a bit of weight. ☐
14. I think she must be getting ill. ☐
15. If you're hungry, there's some leftover food in the fridge. ☐
16. He's such a fussy eater. ☐

a. and I'll do the food for you.
b. before you handle the food. That meat's still raw, you know.
c. I suppose I should try and cut down on the amount of junk food I eat.
d. She's gone completely off her food.
e. We're running out of food.
f. He's always picking at his food. It drives me mad!
g. Just reheat it in the microwave if you feel like it.
h. You more or less live on junk food.

5 Food vocabulary

Complete the texts below with the words in the boxes.

1.
going on	lost	put on

A: Have you (a) . . . . weight? You look thinner.

B: No, quite the opposite. I've actually (b) . . . . five kilos in the last month. I'm thinking of (c) . . . . a diet.

2.
health	junk	organic

A: I don't know how you can eat all that (a) . . . . food like burgers and pizzas and stuff like that. I only eat (b) . . . . stuff which is free from chemicals and additives.

B: Because I like it! All that (c) . . . . food you eat is only good for rabbits, not a full-grown man like me!

3.

green	ripe	rotten	tinned

A: Shall I throw these bananas away? They look
(a) ....

B: No, they're not. They're just very (b) ....

A: I can't eat them like that. I like them when
they're still a bit (c) .... Actually, that's a
lie. I only really like (d) .... fruit. That way
you get it just right!

4.

heavy	light	lovely	main

A: That was a (a) .... meal, wasn't it?

B: Yeah, it was great, but I'm not used to having
such a (b) .... meal in the middle of the
day. I'm not going to get any work done this
afternoon! I usually have my (c) .... meal
of the day in the evening. I usually just have a
(d) .... snack for lunch or just skip it
altogether.

5.

balanced	health	raw	special

I always thought I had quite a (a) .... diet.
I used to eat chocolate and sweets, but I ate plenty
of fruit and vegetables too. I made sure I got my
proteins and everything, but then I developed this
medical problem and they've put me on a
(b) .... diet. Apparently, all that stuff was bad
for my (c) .... and I should just eat
(d) .... fish and vegetables.

6 | It should be banned

Match the topics 1–8 to the statements a–h.

1. a violent new film ☐
2. a new medicine ☐
3. hunting tigers ☐
4. dance music ☐
5. a new book ☐
6. cigarette advertising ☐
7. an extremist political party ☐
8. cars in the city centre ☐

a. It should be banned, because it's not been properly
tested.

b. It should be banned, because it encourages young
people to start.

c. They should be banned, because of all the traffic jams
they cause.

d. It should be banned, because some of the chapters in
it are really offensive to some people.

e. It should be banned, because it's a threat to the
government.

f. It should be banned, because they're almost extinct.

g. It should be banned, because it might encourage
people to commit copycat murders.

h. It should be banned, because it's just a terrible noise!

7 | Eating vocabulary

**Complete the sentences below with the words in
the box.**

barbecue	picnic
brunch	side dish
dessert	snacks
lunch	starter
main course	takeaway

1. I think I'm just going to have the soup for my
.... and then maybe the pork and aubergine
for my ....

2. I'm going out for dinner tonight, and I had a big
breakfast, so I'm going to skip ....

3. I'm on a diet, so I'm not supposed to eat any
.... between meals.

4. If the weather's nice on Sunday, we're going to have a
.... in the garden or go to the park for a
....

5. I can't be bothered to cook tonight. Shall we just get
a Chinese .... instead?

6. I'm going to go for the lamb and get a wild salad as a
....

7. I'm going to skip the .... and just have a
coffee.

8. I missed breakfast this morning, so I might pop out at
eleven and get a bit of ....

8 | Eating out in a big group

**It is often quite difficult to order for a large
group of people! In Britain, one person usually
takes charge of the process. Complete the
conversation below with the words in the box.**

allergic	house wine	ready
go for	main course	selection
good	portions	shout
hands up	rather	starter

– Is everyone having a(n) (1) .... ?

– Shall we just get a(n) (2) .... that everyone can
share?

– Yeah, OK. How many shall we get? Five? Six?

– I think five should be plenty. They serve quite big
(3) . . . . here.

– OK. Do people just want to (4) . . . . out what
they'd like?

– How about a plate of hummus?

– Yeah, and the stuffed vine leaves are really nice as well.

– Shall we get some prawns?

– Actually, I'm (5) . . . . to seafood.

– OK. Well, we can order something else. How about
the goat cheese salad?

– Fine. And can we get some beans and some of those
little sausages?

– OK. Is that all right with everyone? And what do
people want to drink? Is wine OK?

– Yeah.

– Actually, I'd (6) . . . . have beer.

– Yeah, so would I.

– OK. Well (7) . . . . those who want wine. All
right, that's six. Shall we get a couple of bottles?

– Yeah, we can always order some more later if it's not
enough.

– OK. And what do you want? Red or white?

– Red.

– Red.

– OK. Two bottles of red, then. Shall we just get the
(8) . . . . ? And then is it three for beer?

– Actually, I'm just having a Coke. I don't drink.

– OK, then. Has everyone decided what they're having
for their (9) . . . . ?

– No, I can't make up my mind.

– I know. It's difficult, isn't it? I think I'm going to
(10) . . . . the mixed grill.

– Yeah, that sounds (11) . . . . I think I might
have that too.

– OK, then. Are we (12) . . . . to order?

9 More questions you might ask in a group

**Complete these sentences by putting the words
in brackets in the correct order.**

1. Has anyone got enough room left for dessert
. . . . ? (full / is / or / everyone /
already)

2. Does . . . . ? (want / coffee / a /
anyone)

3. Has . . . . ? (for / the / anyone /
asked / bill)

4. Are . . . . ? (going / the / split / we /
just / to / bill)

5. Is . . . . ? (maths / at / anyone / good)

6. How . . . . ? (it / much / person / is /
each / for)

7. Does . . . . ? (tip / include / that / a)

8. Has everyone paid? . . . . (short /
twenty / still / euros / we're)

Learning tip

Try and write a whole conversation using the
questions in Exercise 9. They are in the order you
would probably use them. Writing dialogues is
probably better practice for your speaking than
writing letters and essays.

10 Should've / shouldn't have

**Complete these sentences with *should've* or
shouldn't have.**

1. You . . . . said that. You've hurt her feelings
now!

2. I can't believe you just sat there and let it happen.
You . . . . said something!

3. Are these flowers for me? Oh, really?
You . . . . ! They're lovely! Thank you so
much.

4. It was wonderful when John resigned.
You . . . . seen the boss's face!

5. I went and saw the play last Friday, but I . . . .
bothered. It was such a waste of money.

6. I got an eighty-pound fine, but it was my own
stupid fault. I . . . . been driving so fast.

7. Why didn't you tell me you were coming to
Leeds? You . . . . e-mailed me or rung
beforehand.

8. A: I feel awful!
B: Well, it's your own fault. You . . . . had so
much wine to drink earlier.

9. We had a really nice time on the picnic.
You . . . . come. You would've enjoyed it.

10. I missed the deadline. I knew I . . . . filled the
form in earlier.

13 Sightseeing

1 Places to visit

Make different places to visit by matching 1–8 to a–h.

1. an amazing theme ☐   a. temple
2. a portrait ☐   b. museum
3. a science ☐   c. market
4. an incredible old Hindu ☐   d. cathedral
5. a small jazz ☐   e. gallery
6. an interesting arts and crafts ☐   f. funfair
7. a huge gothic ☐   g. park
8. a travelling ☐   h. club

Which of the places above probably has ...

9. some beautiful stained glass windows? . . . .

10. a permanent collection of medical instruments? . . . .

11. some great gigs? . . . .

12. some beautiful carvings of Indian gods? . . . .

13. a temporary exhibition of photographs of famous people? . . . .

14. the biggest roller coaster in Europe? . . . .

15. lots of little stalls selling pottery and home-made food? . . . .

16. lots of small rides for kids? . . . .

2 What's it like?

Complete the short conversations below with the words in the box.

arcade	give	like	telling
bargains	know	miss	trap
chance	letting	rip-off	visit

Conversation 1

A: Have you been to that club in the centre of town?

B: No, why? What's it (a) . . . . ?

A: It's a bit of a(n) (b) . . . . , actually. It's ten pounds to get in, and then all the drinks are four or five pounds each! I'd give it a(n) (c) . . . . if I were you.

B: Oh, right. Thanks for letting me (d) . . . .

Conversation 2

A: Have you been to that amusement (a) . . . . on the sea front?

B: No, why? What's it like?

A: It's a bit of a tourist (b) . . . . , to be honest. It's full of holidaymakers wasting all their money. I'd (c) . . . . it a miss if I were you.

B: Oh, right. Thanks for (d) . . . . me know.

Conversation 3

A: Have you been to that street market they have every Saturday?

B: No, why? What's it like?

A: Oh, it's great. You can pick up some real (a) . . . . there. I got this bag there for only eight pounds. It's well worth a(n) (b) . . . .

B: Oh, right. Thanks for (c) . . . . me. I'll go down there when I get the (d) . . . .

3 Questions and answers

Complete these questions that tourists ask by putting the words in brackets into the correct order.

1. Do . . . . ? ☐
   (take / here / you / euros)

2. Do you think . . . . ? ☐
   (could / photo / you / us / a / take / for)

3. Do you know . . . . ? ☐
   (the / way / if / is / Guggenheim / the / to / this / Museum)

4. Are there . . . . ? ☐
   (on / tour / any / guided / places / left / the)

5. Are there . . . . ? ☐
   (the / tonight / any / concert / tickets / left / for)

6. Have you . . . . ? ☐
   (rooms / got / any / available)

7. Could you help me? . . . . ? ☐
   (had / I've / stolen / bag / just / my)

Now match the questions 1–7 above to the responses a–g.

a. No, sorry. I'm afraid we've sold out. You could always try later and see if there are any returns.

b. Sorry. I'm not from round here myself.

c. No, sorry. I'm afraid we're fully booked for tonight. Try the Bed and Breakfast place down the road.

d. Yeah, of course. OK. Say 'Cheese'.

e. I'm afraid not, but there's a bank just around the corner.

f. Oh, no. You'd better report it to the police. Do you want me to ring them for you?

g. You don't need to book. Just meet outside the castle gates at seven.

4 | Weather vocabulary

Complete the short dialogues below with the pairs of words in the box.

cloud over / sunny	raining / pouring down
cloudy / brighten up	stopped / easing off
miserable / soaked	

1. A: What a . . . . day!
   B: I know. It's awful. I got . . . . just walking from the bus stop.

2. A: Has it . . . . raining yet?
   B: No, but I think it's . . . . a bit.

3. A: Is it still . . . . outside?
   B: Yeah, it's . . . .

4. A: What's the weather like outside?
   B: Oh, it's just beginning to . . . .
   A: Typical! It was lovely and . . . . this morning, and I was just about to go out now!

5. A: What's the forecast for tomorrow?
   B: I think it said it's going to be quite dull and . . . . in the morning, but it might . . . . later.
   A: Well, so long as it doesn't rain. I'm going on a picnic tomorrow with Judith and Peter.

Now complete the short dialogues below with the pairs of words in the box.

cold / gets	snow / last
hot / get up to	unbearable / sticky
mild / drops	

6. A: What's the weather going to be like on Sunday?
   B: I think it's going to be really . . . . The forecast said it could even . . . . forty.

7. A: What's the weather going to be like at the weekend?
   B: I think they said it's going to . . . ., but it probably won't . . . .

8. A: What's the weather like in the winter?
   B: It's really . . . . It never really . . . . above about freezing.

9. A: What's the weather like in the winter?
   B: Oh, it's quite . . . . It never . . . . below about fifteen degrees centigrade.

10. A: What's the weather like in the summer?
    B: . . . . ! It's really hot and . . . . It can get up to forty-five degrees. You just have to take cold showers all the time.

5 | I don't know

Put the words in the correct order and make phrases which mean *I don't know*.

1. idea / I / no / 've
   . . . .

2. yet / I / decided / really / haven't
   . . . .

3. sure / still / 'm / I / very / not
   . . . .

4. still / it / in / 'm / minds / about / I / two
   . . . .

5. thought / it / haven't / I / about / really
   . . . .

6. mind / can't / my / I / up / make
   . . . .

6 'll / going to / might

Complete the conversations below with the correct forms of 'll, going to and might.

Conversation 1

A: What are you doing later?

B: I don't know. I (a) .... probably just stay in and tidy up the flat a bit. Why?

A: Well, I (b) .... go to the cinema with Hao Dong. I was wondering if you wanted to come along?

A: Yeah, maybe. What (c) .... see?

B: We haven't really decided yet, to be honest, but I thought we (d) .... go and see the new Lynn Ramsay film. It depends where it's on, though. I don't want to go to the multiplex out of town.

A: Yeah, OK. Sounds good. I've been meaning to see that film for ages.

Conversation 2

A: What (a) .... do after you finish your degree?

B: I really haven't thought about it. The only thing I'm certain of is that I (b) .... go to Goa in August with Gina. We went last year and we had such a good time we decided we'd go back there this year. Apart from that, I've no idea. I guess I (c) .... have to get a job, although there is a slight possibility I (d) .... stay on and do a Master's. It depends how well I do in my finals. Knowing me, I (e) .... probably end up failing all my exams and working in a coffee shop or something. I (f) .... just have to wait and see, I suppose.

Conversation 3

A: What are you doing over Christmas?

B: I (a) .... go and stay in a cottage in Wales for a few days with my brother and sister and their partners and kids. It's a kind of family tradition. What about you?

A: I'm still in two minds about it. We (b) .... probably go and stay with my parents, but it's always so boring! Then again, if we stay here, I (c) .... almost certainly end up having to do all the cooking and washing up and everything, so going away (d) .... be the best idea!

7 Future expressions

Today is Monday the 12th. Using the calendar below decide what the following dates are.

1. the day after tomorrow ....
2. the Tuesday after next ....
3. this coming Saturday ....
4. a week tomorrow ....
5. a week on Friday ....
6. two weeks today ....

A U G U S T						
Monday	Tuesday	Wednesday	Thursday	Friday	Saturday	Sunday
			1	2	3	4
5	6	7	8	9	10	11
12	13	14	15	16	17	18
19	20	21	22	23	24	25
26	27	28	29	30	31	

8 I might ... if ...

Make sentences by matching the beginnings 1–7 to the endings a–g.

1. I might go for a walk later ☐
2. I might go to the cinema later ☐
3. I might go to the beach on Saturday ☐
4. I might do a PhD ☐
5. I might get a part-time job ☐
6. I might go and see John ☐
7. I might go and see the exhibition tomorrow ☐

a. if there's anything decent on.

b. if it's as hot as it is today.

c. if he's around.

d. if I can find one.

e. if there's not a huge queue to get in.

f. if it brightens up a bit this afternoon.

g. if I can get a grant to do it.

9 It depends

Complete the two possible answers to each of the questions below.

1. Are you going to go to University?
   a. I hope so, but it depends .... my grades.
   b. I hope so, but it depends .... I pass my exams.

2. Are you going to the reception this evening?
   a. Probably, but it depends . . . . I get back.
   b. Probably, but it depends . . . . tired I feel.

3. Are you going to go on the guided tour?
   a. I don't know. It depends . . . .
      it costs. Do you know?
   b. I don't know. It depends . . . .
      it takes. Do you know?

4. Are you going to go away in the summer?
   a. Hopefully. It depends . . . . I can find any
      last-minute cheap deals.
   b. Hopefully, but it depends . . . . busy I am at
      work.

10 | Writing: I was wondering

**Read the e-mail from an Australian woman to a
friend who is living in Greece. Complete it with
the phrases in the box.**

> if I could come and visit
> if there's some other problem
> if you could put me up
> if you haven't got space
> if you're not going to be around
> whenever you can

Hi Tina,

Just a quick e-mail to let you know I'm setting off on a
trip round Europe two weeks today and I was
wondering (1) . . . . you in
Thessaloniki? I'm flying into London and I'm going to
stay in England for a couple of weeks with some long-
lost relatives – I've got cousins there who I've never
even met. After that, I'm going to get a rail card and
travel round mainland Europe for a month. I haven't
decided exactly where I'm going, but I'll probably head
down south straightaway. I'll probably need the sun
after being in England! I'm planning to be in Greece
around 15th September, but I can't tell you the exact
date yet – I guess it depends whether I meet any
gorgeous men on the way! Obviously, it'd be great
(2) . . . . , but I can always stay
in a cheap hotel (3) . . . . I know
you said your flat was pretty small. Anyway, I'm going
to try and check my shotmail account quite regularly,
so you can e-mail me there (4) . . . .
or (5) . . . . I'll e-mail you again
nearer the time. By the way, I know you've been around
Europe a bit and I was wondering if you could
recommend any good places to go to? I've heard
Milan's good.

Anyway, drop me a line (6) . . . .
and don't work too hard!

Love,
Beth

**When we want someone to do us a favour or we
think we are asking someone to do something
special for us, we often use the structure: *I was
wondering if you could ...?* We usually explain the
situation first. For example:**

A: I'm really sorry to ask, but I've somehow managed to
leave my wallet at home and I was wondering if you
could lend me a few pounds, just until tomorrow?

B: Yeah, of course. How much do you need? Is ten
pounds enough?

Make sentences by matching 1–6 to a–f.

1. I'm going on holiday next week and ☐
2. I'm moving into my new flat and ☐
3. I'm applying for university and ☐
4. They don't speak any English and ☐
5. I've got to write a letter in English and ☐
6. I'm coming to York for a meeting and ☐

a. I was wondering if you could translate for me?

b. I was wondering if you could correct it for me?

c. I was wondering if you could put me up for a night?

d. I was wondering if you could give me a hand?

e. I was wondering if you could write a reference for
   me?

f. I was wondering if you could look after my dog
   while I'm away?

**Now write your own letter to a friend who lives
abroad and who you'd like to visit while you are
on holiday / on a business trip / travelling. Look
back at the model above and underline any other
useful expressions. Try to remember them. Then
write your own letter without looking at Beth's.**

1 School subjects

Complete the sentences below with the school subjects in the box.

art	IT (information technology)
biology	maths
chemistry	PE (physical education)
geography	physics
history	RE (religious education)

1. I used to love . . . ., because I enjoyed finding out about Islam and Buddhism and Hinduism.

2. I used to love . . . ., because I was really interested in how electricity worked.

3. I used to love . . . ., because I was really into football and running.

4. I used to love . . . ., because I was always really good with computers.

5. I used to love . . . ., because I was always really interested in plants and animals.

6. I never really used to like . . . ., because I was never very creative.

7. I never really used to like . . . ., because I was never very good with numbers.

8. I never really used to like . . . ., because I was hopeless at remembering dates.

9. I never really used to like . . . ., because I was hopeless at remembering capitals and counties and states.

10. I never really used to like . . . ., because I was hopeless at remembering elements and which ones go together.

Which of the subjects above do you think the students are talking about in a–j?

a. We learned how to write basic programs today. . . . .

b. We learned about the civil war today. . . . .

c. We learned how to do portraits today. . . . .

d. We learned how to work out the volume of a cube today. . . . .

e. We dissected a frog today. . . . .

f. We read a bit of the Bible today. . . . .

g. We learned how the continents were made today. . . . .

h. We learned how to make salt today. . . . .

i. We learned how sound travels today. . . . .

j. We played hockey today. . . . .

2 The worst teacher I ever had!

Complete these sentences about a terrible teacher with *always* or *never*:

1. He . . . . used to listen to anything we said!

2. He . . . . used to write clearly on the board.

3. He . . . . used to scream and shout at us!

4. He . . . . used to turn up late for class.

5. He . . . . used to give us back our homework on time.

6. He . . . . used to pick on me and blame me for everything that happened!

7. He . . . . used to give us detentions if we spoke in class.

8. He . . . . used to prepare his lessons properly.

9. He . . . . used to tell us what the correct answers were.

10. We . . . . used to fall asleep in his classes because they were so boring!

3 Punishments

Complete the short text below with the words in the box.

bad fight	expelled	got caught	skipping
detention	given lines	humiliating	suspended

At my school, if we (1) . . . . smoking or (2) . . . . lessons, we used to get (3) . . . . I remember once I had to write 'I will never skip Chemistry class again' five hundred times. When I took it into class the next day, my Chemistry teacher just tore it up into little pieces without even looking at it! It was really (4) . . . . If you misbehaved in class, it was quite common to get a(n) (5) . . . . You'd have to stay behind after school for an hour and maybe clean the classroom or something like that. If you did something more serious, like getting into a(n) (6) . . . . or damaging school property, you'd get (7) . . . . for a week, and if you kept doing the same thing time and time again, in the end, you'd get (8) . . . . and your parents would have to find a new school for you to go to. In the whole time I was at school, I think maybe only two or three kids got kicked out, though.

4 Verb patterns

Look back at the words on page 99 of the Coursebook. Did you notice the patterns that followed each verb?

Complete these sentences with the same patterns using the ideas in brackets. The first two are done for you.

1. He's always complaining *to me about the mess in the kitchen*., but he's really untidy himself. (me / the mess in the kitchen)

2. He was sacked *for being drunk at work*., but they still gave him a reference. (be drunk at work)

3. I was once caught . . . . It was really embarrassing. (steal a book from a library)

4. They blamed . . . ., but it wasn't my fault. (me / the incident)

5. He actually threatened . . . . if I didn't give him the money. It was terrifying. (shoot me)

6. He carried on . . . . even though he'd broken his nose. (play)

7. He made . . . ., so you mustn't say anything. (me / swear not to tell anyone)

8. He threatened . . . . if I was late again, so I've bought a louder alarm clock! (me / the sack)

9. They always blame . . . ., but I blame the parents. (teachers / children's bad behaviour)

10. I was caught . . . ., so I had to pay a ten-pound fine. (travel without a ticket)

11. He was sacked . . . . He was really creepy. I hated him. (sexually harass / his secretary)

12. I complained . . . ., but they didn't do anything about him. (the school / several times / our teacher)

5 How did your exam go?

Complete the sentences below with the words in the box.

cheating	none
expecting	passed
messed	re-taking
mind	revision
most	scraped

1. Not very well. I really . . . . up the last two questions.

2. Not very well. I should've done more . . . . for it.

3. Not very well. My . . . . just went completely blank in the middle of it.

4. OK, I suppose. I should've just about . . . . through it.

5. Fine. . . . . of the questions I was expecting came up.

6. Terrible. . . . . of the questions I was expecting came up.

7. Fine. It was much easier than I was . . . .

8. Terrible. I got caught . . . . !

9. Terrible. I'll probably end up . . . . it!

10. Fine. I'm pretty sure I've . . . .

6 How did it go?

Complete the sentences below with the pairs of words in the box.

class / great	interview / really well
class / OK	interview / terribly
driving test / great	meeting / don't ask
exam / OK, I think	meeting / great

1. A: How did the . . . . go?
   B: . . . . I answered most of the questions reasonably well. Now I just have to wait for the results.

2. A: How did the . . . . go?
   B: . . . . ! They asked some really tricky questions and I just mumbled some rubbish. I doubt I got the job.

3. A: How did the . . . . go?
   B: . . . . It was really interesting. The teacher's brilliant!

4. A: How did the .... go?
   B: .... ! We were there for about three hours and we didn't decide anything.

5. A: How did the .... go?
   B: .... ! I passed! I couldn't believe it. I was so nervous beforehand.

6. A: How did the .... go?
   B: .... It was very useful. We sorted out most of the problems we'd been having.

7. A: How did the .... go?
   B: .... They offered me a place straight afterwards, so I'll be starting the MBA in September.

8. A: How did the .... go?
   B: .... The students are quite nice, but we didn't get through as much as I wanted to.

7 | Studying at university

Complete the three texts below with the words in the boxes.

1.

| essays | finals | presentation | term | tutorial |

I'm in the third year of my business management degree, and it's starting to get really stressful. I've got my (a) .... next spring and to be honest, I'm dreading them! On top of that, I've got to write three more (b) .... before Christmas and then five more in the spring (c) ....; I've got to give a(n) (d) .... on marketing strategies next Wednesday and then I've got a(n) (e) .... with my personal tutor the day after to discuss how I'm getting on!

2.

| deadline | dissertation | handouts | lectures |

I'm doing my master's degree at the moment and I'm about halfway through the 20,000-word (a) .... I have to write. The (b) .... for it isn't until next September, so I've still got plenty of time to get it finished. I go to two or three (c) .... a week, and have to take lots of notes. They usually give us a few (d) .... as well, which help to summarise what they've been talking about, so that's helpful.

3.

| coursework | fees | grant | options | specialise |

I'm studying fashion at a big college in Liverpool. I'm quite lucky because I get a(n) (a) .... from the government and all my (b) .... are also paid for. Otherwise, I could never afford to study! In my second year, I can select three particular (c) ...., and I think I'll probably try to (d) .... in shoe design. The other great thing about my degree is that I don't have to take any exams. Everything's based on the (e) .... I do over the whole three years.

Underline any collocations that are new for you.

8 | What are you studying?

Complete the collocations with the words in the box.

| design | engineering | history | studies |

a. ....
   electrical ... , civil ... , computer ... , chemical ... , mechanical ...

b. ....
   graphic ... , web ... , product ... , interior ... , furniture ... , industrial ...

c. ....
   ancient ... , modern ... , European ... , art ... , Chinese language and ...

d. ....
   American ... , media ... , African ... , business ... , Asian ...

Now complete these sentences with words from the lists above.

1. I'm doing .... design. I'm hoping to get a job with a magazine, doing their layouts and things like that.
2. I'm doing .... engineering. I can't wait to finish. I'm looking forward to actually getting out there and building roads and bridges and things.
3. I'm doing .... engineering. I'm planning to do a master's degree in car design when I've finished.
4. I'm doing .... studies. I'm hoping to get into TV or film when I've finished, but there's a lot of competition.
5. I'm doing .... design. Ideally, I want to work for a company like IKEA, which makes lots of different objects – anything from spoons to curtains to sofas.
6. I'm doing .... history. I've no idea what I want to do. I'll probably end up teaching Latin or Greek.

7. I'm doing . . . . studies. I'm applying for management training in all the top companies.

8. I'm doing . . . . history. I'm thinking of going into politics, so it's important to know recent history.

9. I'm doing . . . . studies. I've always been interested in it, because my dad's Nigerian. I'm planning to do a Master's and I'm thinking of maybe doing a PhD after that.

9 | Tests and exams

Make sentences by matching the beginnings 1–8 to the endings a–h.

1. I didn't do very well in my end-of-year exams, ☐
2. I had to take a special entrance exam ☐
3. I failed my medical test to join the army. ☐
4. I did a pregnancy test this morning and ☐
5. They did a blood test, but luckily, ☐
6. I hate having oral exams. ☐
7. He failed the drugs test after the race, ☐
8. The police stopped me and did a breath test. ☐

a. in order to get into university. It was really difficult.
b. They said I wasn't fit enough to fight.
c. so I'm going to have to re-take several in September.
d. so they took away his gold medal and banned him from all future competitions.
e. I can never speak properly when I'm under pressure.
f. I don't know why. I was driving perfectly normally and I hadn't been drinking.
g. everything came up negative, so I haven't got any nasty diseases!
h. it was positive! I'm going to have a baby!

10 | Plans and hopes

Make sentences by matching the beginnings 1–7 to the endings a–g.

1. I'm planning ☐
2. I'm expecting ☐
3. I'm hoping ☐
4. I'm looking forward to ☐
5. I'm dreading ☐
6. I'm applying ☐
7. I'm thinking ☐

a. going on the plane as I'm scared of flying.
b. I get the job.
c. of getting a new computer.
d. visitors later, so don't come round.
e. for several jobs at the moment.
f. having a holiday.
g. to visit some relations while I'm in Australia.

11 | Short natural answers

Choose the correct words.

1. A: What do you think the weather'll be like tomorrow?
   B: *It'll probably / It'll hopefully* rain again. It's always horrible and cold and wet at this time of year.

2. A: Do you think you'll ever speak English like a native speaker?
   B: *I'm bound to / I doubt it.* You need to live in a country where they speak English if you want to get that good.

3. A: Do you think you'll ever get married?
   B: *Definitely / Hopefully.* I mean, it depends whether or not I meet the right person, but I'd like to.

4. A: Do you think you'll ever do a PhD?
   B: *I doubt it / Probably.* Doing my master's degree nearly killed me, so I've had enough of studying, really.

5. A: Do you think you'll carry on studying English after this course?
   B: *I doubt it / I might.* It depends how much free time I have, of course, but if I can, I'll try to.

6. A: Do you think they'll ever find life on other planets?
   B: *Probably / They might.* I mean, there's so many millions of planets out there, there must be life somewhere.

7. A: Do you think your country will win the next World Cup?
   B: *Definitely / Hopefully.* I'll be delighted if they do. I'm praying for it already!

8. A: Do you think you'll live to be a hundred?
   B: *Hopefully not / Definitely.* Imagine being that old and frail. It'd be horrible!

15 Sport

1 Do, play or go?

Complete these sentences with the correct form of do, play or go.

1. My son's thirteen now, and loves . . . . skate-boarding in the local parks.

2. When I was younger, my brother and I used to . . . . table tennis all the time!

3. People have only really started . . . . football in my country since the last World Cup.

4. I go to the gym quite a lot because I . . . . a lot of aerobics there.

5. I'm . . . . skiing in Iran this winter. It should be really good fun.

6. If you're feeling stiff, you should try . . . . a bit of yoga. It's great for keeping you supple.

7. When I was at school, we used to have to . . . . rugby all through the winter. It was horrible!

8. When I was a kid, my dad and I used to . . . . fishing every Sunday morning.

9. Do you understand how to . . . . cricket? It's such a strange game!

10. Listen, we're all . . . . bowling tomorrow night and I was wondering if you wanted to come along?

11. My daughter . . . . karate every Wednesday after school. She'll be a brown belt soon.

12. My brother's a keep-fit fanatic. He . . . . cycling every night. He usually does about forty miles!

13. I used to be really good at athletics when I was at school. I used to . . . . the high jump really well.

14. I can't believe it! My dad's actually started . . . . golf recently!

15. She got mugged a few months ago, and since then she's started . . . . boxing as a kind of self-defence thing.

2 Are you any good?

Match the sports 1–8 comments a–h.

1. football ☐
2. golf ☐
3. karate ☐
4. running ☐
5. snow-boarding ☐
6. surfing ☐
7. swimming ☐
8. tennis ☐

a. I'm quite good at doing the breast stroke, but I can't do the butterfly at all!

b. I'm quite good at dribbling, but I'm terrible at tackling. I'm scared of hurting my legs!

c. I'm OK for a beginner, but I still can't ride really big waves.

d. My forehand's quite good, but my serve's terrible. I sometimes lose a whole game with double faults!

e. I'm quite good at sprinting, but I'm useless over longer distances.

f. I'm fine going downhill and off-piste, but I can't do any tricks or jumps.

g. I'm quite good at putting, but my drive's terrible – I always hit the ball miles off the fairway.

h. I'm OK. I'm a brown belt at the moment.

3 Win or beat?

Complete these phrases with win or beat.

1. . . . . three–two
2. . . . . Brazil four–one
3. . . . . three silver medals
4. . . . . the European record
5. . . . . the champions
6. . . . . the World Cup
7. . . . . a competition
8. . . . . your biggest rivals
9. . . . . the League
10. . . . . the favourite
11. . . . . a set (in tennis)
12. . . . . your own fastest time

Now complete these sentences with words from above.

13. I managed to do the whole run in under twenty minutes! That's beaten my fastest . . . . by almost four minutes.

14. It's always crazy in Milan when AC Milan play Inter because they're deadly . . . .

15. A: How did they manage to get a free holiday?

    B: They won a . . . . in a magazine and that was the first prize.

16. She beat the world . . . . for the 1500 metres by about five seconds!

17. They've got a really difficult game on Sunday. They're away to the defending . . . . They only lost two games in the whole of last season.

18. He won the first . . . . six–one, but he's losing the second by five games to three at the moment.

4 Different kinds of games

Complete the sentences below with the words in the box.

card	computer	cup	drinking	team

1. We've got a big . . . . game this weekend. If we win, we're through to the semi-finals.

2. I wish I'd never bought him that PlayStation™. He spends half his life playing . . . . games now!

3. I do like sport. It's just that I can't stand . . . . games. I much prefer things like tennis or athletics.

4. When I was a kid, we always used to play . . . . games like Snap and Happy Families to pass the time on long journeys.

5. A: How was your trip?

    B: Awful! I was taken out for dinner by the local distributor, and then they took me to a bar and made me take part in all these stupid . . . . games!

Now complete the sentences below with the words in the box.

away	ball	board	kids'	season

6. My dad really loves playing . . . . games like chess and Monopoly.

7. They're at home tomorrow, and then they've got three . . . . games in a row, which will be tough.

8. I've always been quite good at most . . . . games, but I'm probably best at volleyball.

9. We were on the top of the league for weeks, but we lost the championship on the last game of the . . . .

10. One of the most popular . . . . games in my country is called 'It'. One person is 'It' and they have to chase everyone else and then the first person they touch becomes 'It'.

5 More first conditionals

Complete these conversations with the correct form of the words in brackets.

Conversation 1

A: Have you heard that Andrew's thinking of going to work in China for a year?

B: I know! I can't believe it. He (a) . . . . (not be able to) speak to anyone there if he (b) . . . . (do).

A: I don't know. He's quite good with languages. I'm sure he (c) . . . . (be able to) pick up bits and pieces.

B: I hope you're right because if he (d) . . . . (not do), he (e) . . . . (be) very lonely.

Conversation 2

A: Did you know that Maria's thinking of leaving her husband because he's been having an affair, and she's going to take the baby with her.

B: Really? She must be mad. How (a) . . . . (she / be able to) look after it if she (b) . . . . (do) that?

A: I don't know, but I'm sure she (c) . . . . (work something out). It (d) . . . . (be) worse for the baby if she (e) . . . . (stay).

Conversation 3

A: Did Tina tell you she's thinking of becoming a teacher?

B: Yeah, but it (a) . . . . (be) a disaster if she (b) . . . . (do).

A: Why? The money (c) . . . . (be) OK and she (d) . . . . (meet) lots of interesting people.

B: Yeah , and she (e) . . . . (have to) stay at work until midnight and work weekends and everything. And all the kids (f) . . . . (probably / give) her a nervous breakdown!

Conversation 4

A: I heard that Sharon's thinking of dropping out of
university.

B: I know. She must be mad! It (a) . . . . (ruin) her
career chances if she (b) . . . . (do).

A: Do you think so? Personally, I think she should do it.
She (c) . . . . (not get) a good grade if she
(d) . . . . (not be) happy with what she's
studying.

B: Maybe, but if she (e) . . . . (drop out) now, how
(f) . . . . (she / pay) her rent and all her bills?

A: I don't know. She (g) . . . . (find) a way
somehow.

6 Expressions with *if*

**Complete the eight *if*- expressions below with
the words in the box.**

don't	hand	might	see
give	let	rather	tell

1. I'll . . . . her if I see her.
2. I'll . . . . if I can.
3. If I hear the result, I'll . . . . you a ring.
4. I . . . . do it later if I feel like it.
5. I'll go if I really have to, but I'd . . . . not.
6. I'll give you a . . . . if you want.
7. We . . . . have to buy it if you don't like it.
8. I'll . . . . you have it if I can find it.

**Now use the *if*- expressions above to complete
a–h below.**

a. A: I've got to work this afternoon, so I'm going to
miss the Wimbledon semi-finals.

   B: Oh, no! Well, listen, ... at the
office, OK?

b. A: That looks really heavy. Are you OK with it?
. . . .

   B: It's all right. I'll be OK, but thanks for offering.

c. A: Oh, no! I've just realised that Sheila doesn't know
that the class this afternoon has been cancelled.

   B: Oh really? Well, ... and maybe
we should ask everyone else to do the same.

d. I'm still not sure if I'll be able to make tomorrow
night. It all depends how busy I am. Anyway,
. . . . , but don't be too surprised
if I don't.

e. A: Have you had a look at the heater yet?

   B: No, not yet. Give me a chance. I've only just got
home from work. , but I'm
not promising anything.

f. A: Have you got that hammer I lent you here?

   B: Yeah, somewhere, but I'm not sure where exactly.
I'll have to look for it later. ,
OK?

g. A: You can't change your mind now. I've told my
mother that you're coming! She'll be really
disappointed if you don't.

   B: Well, ... You know what
I think of your parents!

h. A: I know I said I liked the Renault yesterday, but
I've been having second thoughts.

   B: Don't worry! . . . . I've gone off
it too! I think we should go for the Audi. What
do you think?

7 He should've scored that!

**When we talk about football matches or other
sporting events, we often use *should've* to talk
about things we wanted to happen, but which
didn't, and *shouldn't have* to talk about things we
didn't want to happen, but which did. Match 1–5
to a–e.**

1. He should've saved it, ☐
2. He should've been sent off, ☐
3. He should've scored, ☐
4. We should've won, ☐
5. We should've lost, ☐

a. but we missed two penalties!
b. but the referee just gave him a yellow card.
c. because they had a lot of good chances.
d. but he hit the post.
e. but he let it go through his legs!

Now match 6–10 to f–j.

6. He should've won the race, ☐
7. She should've won the match. ☐
8. He shouldn't have been in the race. ☐
9. He should've won that point, ☐
10. She should've won the race, ☐

f. but he put the volley into the net.
g. but his engine caught fire with two laps to go.
h. but she tripped and fell on the last lap.
i. She was a set up and leading 4–1 in the second.
j. He failed a drugs test a few weeks ago.

8 I know / I don't know

Complete the conversations below by adding I know or I don't know.

1. A: There's too much sport on TV these days.
    B: . . . . If people want to watch it, it's up to them, isn't it?

2. A: That was a great game!
    B: . . . . ! I nearly had a heart attack when we got that last-minute try.

3. A: Politicians don't care about us.
    B: . . . . They're only in it for the money and the fame.

4. A: Philosophy is such a pointless subject.
    B: . . . . It doesn't exactly help you get a job, does it?

5. A: I can't believe how badly doctors get paid.
    B: . . . . I think they do OK, especially compared to what I'm earning!

6. A: The traffic in town is impossible these days.
    B: . . . . It used to be worse before they introduced the new one-way system.

7. A: The countryside's much nicer in the north.
    B: . . . . It depends where you go, doesn't it?

8. A: Sportsmen get paid too much these days.
    B: . . . . Someone's got to make some money from sport, and I'd rather it was the people who actually played it than their agent.

9. A: I don't know why people like her so much.
    B: . . . . Who does she think she is?

10. A: I don't know what he thinks he's doing, driving around in a car like that.
    B: . . . . I think he looks kind of cool in it myself.

9 Writing

Complete the e-mails asking about different sports and keep-fit classes, with the words in the box.

available	keen	run
exact	necessary	told
grateful	recommended	wondering
interested		

Dear Sir/Madam,

A friend of mine (1) . . . . me that you are going to be running a t'ai-chi course at your gym this autumn. I'm really (2) . . . . in joining this course, and I was (3) . . . . if you could tell me the (4) . . . . dates the course will be starting and finishing? I would also like to know the days and times it will (5) . . . .

Many thanks,

Danny Hocker

Dear Sir/Madam,

A friend of mine (6) . . . . a kick-boxing course that you run and I am very (7) . . . . to enrol for the next course providing you still have places (8) . . . . I am afraid I am a complete beginner, and would therefore be (9) . . . . if you would let me know whether any experience is (10) . . . . I was also wondering if you could confirm the exact cost of the course and the methods of payment?

I look forward to hearing from you soon,

Yours

Anna Lingstrom

Now write an e-mail to a gym/sports centre asking about a forthcoming course that you are interested in joining. Tell them how you heard about the course. Ask about some of the following:

*   the dates
*   the days and times
*   the cost
*   if any experience is necessary
*   if you'll need any special equipment

Use the two e-mails above as models if you need to. The following sentence starters will help you:

I would be grateful if you could tell me ...
I was wondering if you could confirm/let me know ...
I would also like
    to know when/how much/if/whereabouts exactly ...

1 What kind of business?

Complete the sentences below with the words in the box.

designing	myself
exporting	producing
family	provides
firm	sells
multinational	specialises

1. I work for a big . . . . company which has offices all over the world.

2. I work for the . . . . business as my father's personal assistant.

3. I work for . . . . I'm a plumber.

4. I work for a(n) . . . . of consultants which provides software solutions to businesses.

5. I work for a voluntary organisation which . . . . help and advice for the blind.

6. I work for a small firm of architects which specialises in . . . . schools.

7. I work for a big law firm which . . . . in company law.

8. I have a small specialist bookshop which only . . . . publications on sport.

9. I run my own business importing and . . . . rice.

10. I run my own business . . . . machines for the car industry.

2 Problems, problems!

The verbs in the box collocate with _problem_. Use them in the correct form to complete the sentences below.

cause	deal with	get worse	ignore	sort out

1. Pollution is a major problem in our country which is just . . . . and worse because the government has no policies to . . . . it.

2. Our company usually transports goods by train, so this railway strike has . . . . us a lot of problems.

3. It's taken us a long time to . . . . the problems with our computer system, but it seems to be running smoothly now.

4. The big boss has known our branch has been in a mess for ages, but he's just been . . . . the problem, because our manager is his son!

Language note

With many phrasal verbs, when you use an object pronoun you have to put it between the verb and the particle:
I need to <u>sort</u> it <u>out</u>.
<u>Look</u> it <u>up</u> in a dictionary.
They <u>put up</u> their prices last month and they've <u>put them up</u> again this month.

However, some phrasal verbs like _deal with_ can't be divided in this way:
I don't know what to do about the problem. Can you <u>deal with</u> it?
Tom's wedding should be good. I'm really <u>looking forward to</u> it.
Is she <u>going out with</u> him? I saw them holding hands yesterday.

There are no easy rules to remember which phrasal verbs can be divided and which can't. This is just another reason why you need to notice and record good examples of how phrasal verbs are used!

3 More problems

Complete the sentences below with the adjectives in the box.

admin	marital
behavioural	mental health
financial	social
health	technical

1. My brother and his wife are talking about getting divorced. They've been having a lot of . . . . problems.

2. Jim's a really heavy drinker and a heavy smoker, too, so it's not surprising he's got . . . . problems, really.

3. He had really serious . . . . problems and had to start seeing a psychiatrist about things.

4. The government hasn't done enough to sort out all the . . . . problems here like drug addiction and homelessness.

5. The National Theatre lost £6 million last year. They're having really serious . . . . problems.

6. I don't know why, but I've been having a few . . . . problems with my Internet server recently.

7. They said they'd lost my application because they've got a new secretary. They've been having a few . . . . problems.

8. He's been getting into lots of fights and arguing with teachers. They say he's got . . . . problems.

4 Collocations: *company* and *business*

Complete the sentences below with the words in the box.

car	do	keep	mind	partner
design	good	losing	news	policy

1. We . . . . a lot of business in Spain and Italy.

2. I'll have to talk to my business . . . . about your offer before I can make any decisions.

3. The dollar is so strong at the moment that we're . . . . a lot of business.

4. They gave me a company . . . . at work, because I have to travel quite a bit.

5. I work in the suburbs of town for this little . . . . company.

6. Sorry, but you're not allowed to send personal e-mails from the office. It's against company . . . .

7. What do you think about this business in the . . . . about the rioting in the capital?

8. Are you going out? Is it OK if I come along, just to . . . . you company?

9. Don't you know Nan-Joo? She's got a great sense of humour. She's very . . . . company.

10. I asked her if she had a boyfriend, and she told me to . . . . my own business!

Underline any *business/company* collocations in the sentences above that are new for you. Why are examples 7, 8, 9, and 10 different from the others?

5 How's business?

Look at the replies below to the question, 'How's business?' Then, based on each reply 1–14, write *Great*, *Bad* or *Just OK* on the line.

1. . . . . We're really struggling.

2. . . . . We're doing all right <u>at the moment</u>.

3. . . . . Business is booming.

4. . . . . We've made a big profit <u>this year</u>.

5. . . . . We've made a big loss <u>this year</u>.

6. . . . . We're breaking even <u>at the moment</u>.

7. . . . . We've already lost two of our biggest customers <u>so far this year</u>.

8. . . . . We've had a lot of new orders <u>recently</u>.

9. . . . . We haven't been too badly affected by the recession <u>so far</u>.

10. . . . . We're going to open two new branches <u>in the next year</u>, so we're expanding quite quickly.

11. . . . . We've taken on ten new people <u>since last year</u>, so we're expanding quite quickly.

12. . . . . We've had to get rid of twenty people <u>so far this year</u>.

13. . . . . We're going to have to cut costs drastically <u>over the next year</u>.

14. . . . . We've had so much work <u>recently</u> we've actually had to turn some down!

Which of the underlined time phrases above go with:

a. the present perfect?

b. the present continuous?

c. *going to* + verb?

Learning tip

Whenever you do an exercise like Exercise 5, it's important to try to notice collocations. You can do the following task anytime: Write down the key words below. Cover the text. Try and remember the collocations. For example, can you remember the collocations from Exercise 5 above for the following?

business	*profit*
loss	*branches*
new people	*twenty people*
costs	*work*

Now look back at the sentences in Exercise 5 and check if you were right or not.

6 | Business verbs

Complete the texts below with the correct form of the verbs in the boxes.

1.

launch	modify	re-launch	withdraw

A few years ago, a famous car company had to
(a) . . . . their new model soon after it was
(b) . . . . because they found out it was unsafe
when it went round corners at speed. After they
(c) . . . . it, the car was (d) . . . . and is
now quite successful.

2.

raise	receive	reduce	re-think	set

A few years ago, British Airways decided to focus on
the business and luxury travel market. They
(a) . . . . the numbers of seats on their planes
and (b) . . . . prices substantially. They
(c) . . . . a lot of complaints about the strategy.
Then the market was hit by September 11ᵗʰ. Since
then, they have been forced to (d) . . . . prices
and (e) . . . . them lower.

3.

choose	develop	interrupt	start	wreck

When I left university, I had a couple of ideas about
what I wanted to do, and in the end I (a) . . . .
to go into publishing. When I (b) . . . . my
career, there weren't many women at the top of the
company and it was almost impossible to
(c) . . . . your career to have children. I was
always quite ambitious, so I decided to
(d) . . . . my career rather than start a family.
I don't regret it for a minute. I was made managing
director last year. I get to travel round the world
and I have the money to do more or less what
I want. Having a baby would've (e) . . . . all that.

7 | Important expressions

Complete the sentences below with the words in the box.

housing	petrol	reduce	schools
increase	recession	risen	weak

1. Inflation has . . . . by twelve percent in the last six months. It's a bit worrying.

2. I only get three pounds an hour at work, but I don't have to worry about my rent because I get . . . . benefit.

3. I can't believe it! They've actually decided to . . . . taxes by ten percent! I'll save a fortune!

4. The dollar is really . . . . at the moment, so it's a good time to buy stuff from America.

5. I wish the government would spend less on the military and start investing more in . . . . and hospitals.

6. Unemployment is on the . . . . at the moment. It went up by something like five hundred thousand last month.

7. The economy is in . . . . I can't see things getting any better for at least the next five years.

8. I can't really afford to drive to work any more, because the tax on . . . . is so high at the moment!

8 | Promises, promises!

Make promises the government made before the last election by matching 1–4 to a–d.

1. They said they were going to cut
2. They said they were going to create
3. They said they were going to make
4. They said they were going to protect

a. the environment,
b. it easier for people to buy their own homes,
c. thousands of new jobs,
d. taxes,

Now match 5–8 to e–h.

5. They said they were going to build ☐ ☐
6. They said they were going to ban ☐ ☐
7. They said they were going to do more to tackle ☐ ☐
8. They said they were going to provide ☐ ☐

e. street crime,
f. better health care,
g. hundreds of new schools,
h. cigarette advertising,

Now complete sentences 1–8 by matching i–viii.

i. but unemployment's higher than it's ever been now!
ii. but hundreds of doctors are leaving the health service every year!
iii. but there's still lots of muggings round where we live!
iv. but they've just signed a deal to let an oil company drill just off the coast here!
v. but they haven't yet. I think they must be funded by the big tobacco companies!
vi. but the one my daughter goes to is in a terrible state! They should do that up first!
vii. but there's no way someone like me could get a mortgage.
viii. but they still take 40% out of your wages every month, don't they?

9 First and second conditionals

We usually use first conditional when we think things are going to happen or that they're possible. We usually use the second conditional when we are sure they won't happen or that they're impossible.

Complete these sentences with the correct form of the verbs in brackets. Decide if a first or second conditional is better.

1. I'm not going to take that job. If I . . . . , I . . . . move house. (do, have to)
2. I . . . . with him if he . . . . the last man on earth! (not go out, be)
3. I'm applying for a job in Italy. If I . . . . it, I . . . . in September. (get, start)
4. I can't see myself ever working abroad, but if I . . . . , I . . . . and live in the States. (do, go)
5. Sorry, I'm really short of money. I . . . . you some money if I . . . . , but I just don't have enough. (lend, can)

6. I might go out later, I suppose, but if there . . . . anything good on TV, then I . . . . instead. (be, stay in)
7. They'll never win. I . . . . absolutely delighted if they . . . . , but it won't happen. (be, do)
8. I'm getting the early bus, so I . . . . you if I . . . . home before eleven. (ring, get)
9. You're doing a marathon? You must be mad! I . . . . one even if you . . . . me! (not do, pay)
10. They'll never change the law to lower the speed limit to 90 km per hour on the motorway. If they . . . . , everybody . . . . it. (do, ignore)

10 Grammar: *would* or *'ll*

Complete these sentences with *would* or *'ll*.

1. I . . . . get it for you. I'm going to the shops anyway.
2. I . . . . help, but I'm in a rush.
3. I . . . . tell him. I'm going to see him later.
4. I . . . . look for it later. I should be back quite early.
5. I . . . . normally see him, but I'm not going into the office today.
6. I . . . . fix it, but I don't have the right tools.
7. I . . . . come, but I've got a meeting tomorrow.
8. I . . . . see. It depends how busy I am.
9. I . . . . wait and see if I were you. It might be busy.
10. I . . . . do it if you like. I'm not doing anything this afternoon.
11. I . . . . n't be seen dead in a place like that!
12. I . . . . do it one day. You just wait.

17 Friends and family

1 Relationships

Complete the sentences below with the words in the box. You will only need to use some of the words.

aunts	girlfriend	niece
boyfriend	half-brother	step-brother
cousins	half-sister	step-mother
ex	mother-in-law	step-sister
father-in-law	nephew	uncles

1. I'm going to become an uncle for the first time next month. My sister's expecting a baby girl. She'll be my . . . .

2. We went out for almost five years, but we just gradually grew apart. We were only sixteen when we started going out. It was quite amicable when we broke up, and I still see him occasionally for a drink. He's my . . . .

3. We were very close when we were younger. My brothers and I were of a similar age to them, and they lived just round the corner, so we used to hang around with each other all the time. Since we moved away, we don't see each other so often. I think the last time was at my aunt's fiftieth birthday party. They are my . . . .

4. He's my mum's son from her first marriage. He's quite a lot older, but we've always got on fine. He used to play with me and take me out all the time. I think he liked having a baby sister. He's my . . . .

5. It was difficult at first. I think she was often quite critical of me. I don't think any woman could ever be quite good enough for her son. Now that we've been married two years, though, we get on really well. She's a very nice woman. We're actually quite similar! She's my . . . .

6. He's really wild. I find it really difficult when my sister brings him round to visit. I find it quite annoying because he might break something, but then my sister won't do anything, and I can't tell him off because my sister will say I'm interfering. The kid's basically a spoilt brat. He's my . . . .

7. We get on a bit better than we used to. He's the same age as me, but we're quite different people. He came to live with us when my dad re-married when I was twelve. I guess we were both competing for attention, as neither of us had any other brothers or sisters, and so we used to fight all the time. He's my . . . .

Match 8–13 to a–f. Did you notice the collocations in 1–7 above?

8. We get on   ☐
9. They're always competing   ☐
10. She's expecting   ☐
11. They hang around   ☐
12. We gradually   ☐
13. We had an amicable   ☐

a. a baby.
b. with each other all the time.
c. better than we used to.
d. break-up.
e. for attention.
f. grew apart.

2 Adjectives and expressions to describe people

Complete the sentences below with the pairs of words in the box.

big-headed / showing off	liberal / let
fussy / please	outgoing / get on with
gorgeous / looks	quiet / says
independent / get	strict / lets

1. My dad's very . . . . He never . . . . me do anything!

2. My parents were quite . . . . They . . . . me do more or less whatever I wanted.

3. His girlfriend's . . . . She . . . . like a model.

4. My little brother's really . . . . He's really difficult to . . . . He's never happy.

5. His wife's so . . . . She hardly . . . . anything. You hardly know she's there.

6. My granddad's very . . . . He's eighty-three, but he still lives on his own and he can still . . . . about by himself.

7. There's an awful guy in my class. He's so . . . . He's always . . . . and he just thinks he's God's gift to women.

8. My mum's very . . . . She's very easy to . . . .

72

3 Know, get to know, meet, make, have

The words above are often confused. Look at the explanations below and complete the typical example sentences by putting the words into the correct form.

1. If you *know* someone, you are familiar with them. We usually use *know* in the present simple or present perfect.
   a. Do you . . . . Andrew?
   b. They . . . . only . . . . each other for four weeks and they've already decided to get married!
   c. I . . . . someone who works there, but I've forgotten her name for the minute. Fiona! That's it!

2. If you *get to know* someone, you find out more about them and become more friendly with them.
   a. A: Bill's very quiet isn't he?
      B: Not really. He's just a bit shy with new people. He's quite chatty once you . . . . him.
   b. I worked with her for years before I . . . . her properly.
   c. We . . . . each other better when we went on the school trip to France.

3. We use *meet* to describe any time you see someone. We don't usually use it in the present simple.
   a. A: Janet, ... you . . . . John before?
      B: No. I don't think so. Hi, John.
   b. It was nice . . . . you.
   c. I . . . . him while I was at university. We were in the same tutor group.
   d. I . . . . Simon and Jo later. Do you want to come?
   e. I . . . . Jean while I was out shopping. I hadn't seen her for ages.
   f. A: How was the party?
      B: Great. I . . . . loads of new people.

4. With the word *friend*, we often use the verbs *make, have,* or *be*.
   a. It's difficult to . . . . new friends when you live in a big city.
   b. I . . . . n't really . . . . any friends since I've been here.
   c. I . . . . a friend who works there. She's called Lindsay Davies. Do you know her?
   d. I . . . . a friend who lives in Munich, so I'm going to stay with her.
   e. This is John. He . . . . a friend of mine from university.

f. A: This is Ben. I guess he must . . . . my oldest friend. How long have we known each other? Thirty years?
   B: Yeah, something like that.

4 Present perfect and past simple

Complete these sentences with *I've known her* or *I met her*.

1. . . . . since I was a child.
2. . . . . longer than anyone.
3. . . . . while I was on holiday.
4. . . . . for ages, but we're not really friends.
5. . . . . while I was working in Starbucks.
6. . . . . just recently.
7. . . . . ever since I can remember.
8. . . . . for the first time at school.

5 Relationship verbs

Match the comments 1–6 to the responses a–f.

1. I've fancied her for ages. ☐
2. Are those two going out now? ☐
3. I'm going to meet her parents. ☐
4. I'm sorry. It's not you, it's me. I'm just not ready to settle down yet. ☐
5. Have Gary and Lesley split up or something? I haven't seen them together for a while. ☐
6. I've just seen Anna with Tom. I thought she was with someone else now. ☐

a. Really? It must be getting serious, then.
b. You mean you didn't know? They've been an item for about six months now. It's old news!
c. Didn't you hear? She was seeing someone behind his back, and he's left her.
d. She was, but it didn't work out with the other guy, and so they've got back together.
e. Well, why don't you ask her out, then?
f. Why not? Have you met someone else?

6 | Second conditionals

We often comment on other people's relationships by using *would* or a second conditional sentence. For example:
I don't know why she puts up with him! I wouldn't.

Complete these sentences. Put the verbs in brackets into either the *would* form or the past simple.

1. I . . . . (never / say) anything so awful to my girlfriend! She'd kill me!

2. I . . . . (never / do) anything like that to him. He'd never forgive me!

3. I . . . . (never / go out) with anyone who . . . . (look) like that. What would my friends say?

4. I . . . . (never / go out) with anyone who . . . . (treat) me so badly. Neither would you!

5. I . . . . (tell) him to get lost if he . . . . (do) that to me.

6. If my boyfriend . . . . (take) me for granted like that, I . . . . (dump) him.

7. I don't know what I . . . . (do) if I . . . . (find out) my girlfriend had been cheating on me. I . . . . (probably / just / try) and pretend it hadn't happened.

8. I don't know what I . . . . (do) if she . . . . (leave) me. I . . . . (probably / have) a nervous breakdown.

9. I don't know what I . . . . (do) if anything like that . . . . (happen) to me. I . . . . (probably / go mad) and kill someone.

10. What would you do if you . . . . (find out) your girlfriend . . . . (be) pregnant? I think I . . . . (faint)!

7 | Guessing and being vague

Complete the dialogue below with the words and expressions in the box.

a bit	some kind of
can't	something to do with
must (x2)	think
reckon	wonder
seems	

A: What do you (1) . . . . of her new boyfriend?

B: I don't know. I didn't talk to him that much, but he (2) . . . . nice enough – (3) . . . . dull, though.

A: Yeah, I thought he was quite boring too. How old do you (4) . . . . he is?

B: I don't know, but he (5) . . . . be quite a lot older than she is. I don't know – late thirties, early forties.

A: Yeah, at least. I (6) . . . . what she sees in him.

B: Well, it (7) . . . . be his looks, can it? Let's be honest, he's fairly ugly, isn't he? Did you see the car he was driving, though? He (8) . . . . be loaded.

A: I guess so. What does he do?

B: He did tell me, but I wasn't really listening. It's (9) . . . . finance. He's (10) . . . . accountant or something like that.

Underline the whole phrases using the ten words and expressions. Notice the grammar that goes with them.

8 | Talking about recent history

Complete the sentences below with the words and expressions in the box.

a big recession	a very exciting time
a civil war	in power
a dictatorship	independence
a huge economic boom	the end of the cold war
a social revolution	

1. There was . . . . in the early nineties. There was a stock market crash and massive unemployment.

2. There was . . . . in the fifties between the North and the South. Over a million people died.

3. Our country gained . . . . at the beginning of the sixties. We were a British colony before that.

4. The Conservatives were .... during the late nineties. The less said about that, the better.

5. There was .... in the seventies. Women became a lot more liberated.

6. There was .... in the mid-eighties. There was a lot of foreign investment and lots of people got very rich.

7. We saw .... in the late eighties and early nineties after the Berlin Wall came down.

8. We were living under .... in the sixties and seventies. Things were very difficult, and there were a lot of human rights abuses.

9. The late eighties was ...., culturally. There were a lot of great bands and films around then.

9 | I used to, but I don't any more

Match the statements about the past 1–8 to the reasons why something stopped a–h.

1. We used to live next door to each other, ☐
2. We used to be really close, ☐
3. I never used to get on with my brother, ☐
4. I never used to think I wanted kids, ☐
5. I used to love football, ☐
6. I used to love driving, ☐
7. I used to love dogs, ☐
8. I used to want to be a doctor, ☐

a. but we've been a lot closer since our dad died.

b. but since I turned thirty, I've really started thinking about it.

c. but I went off it after I broke my ankle playing it!

d. but I went off them after one bit me once.

e. but I went off the idea after I heard what long hours they work.

f. but she moved away a few years ago.

g. but I went off it after I had a car crash.

h. but we've grown apart over the last few years.

10 | Writing: describing social trends

Complete the text about housing in London with the words and expressions in the box.

a number of factors	over the last few years
a recent report	over the next ten years
continue	significant

According to (1) .... by the Greater London Assembly, London will need to build three million more homes (2) ...., despite the fact that in Britain as a whole, the population is likely to fall. The report suggests the increasing need for housing is due to (3) .... Firstly, the manufacturing industry has declined in the north of England (4) .... and people have moved south to look for work. Secondly, there has been a(n) (5) .... rise in the number of people, particularly women, choosing to live on their own and this trend is expected to (6) .... Finally, more and more marriages are ending in divorce – almost one in three last year – meaning that one of the partners leaves the family home and requires a place of their own.

Now complete each of the following sets of collocations with one or two words from the text.

7. .... a recent survey / statistics published recently / the government.

8. They .... to make changes over the next few months / over the next five years / by 2002.

9. The change is .... the growth of the economy / the decreasing birth rate / several trends.

10. The mining industry .... over the last year / over the last few months / since they came to power.

11. There has been a small / steady / enormous .... in the number of people getting divorced.

12. The number of single-parent families seems certain to .... grow / fall / decline / rise.

Write a short description of trends and changes in your country connected to one of the following:

- family and marriage
- the population
- work
- transport
- housing

You may also want to look back at the model in Unit 3 on page 000 for other ideas.

1 Festivals

Complete the texts below with the words in the boxes.

1.

bands	fantastic parade
street party	outrageous costumes

If you're going to visit Sydney, you should go at the beginning of March, because they have this amazing Mardi Gras festival. I went last year, and it was wild. It was just a huge (a) . . . . – you know, lots of drinking and dancing, and there is a(n) (b) . . . . with dancers and incredible floats with (c) . . . . and sound systems on them, blasting out music. I'll have to show you the photos I took. People dress up in some really (d) . . . .
I met a couple of great guys there. The people are really friendly.

2.

firework displays	go on	going to
is on	letting off	outdoor concerts

Personally, I hate the Fallas festival. I try to get out of Valencia when it (a) . . . . It's just so noisy! They always have (b) . . . . with bands blasting out awful music in the square near my flat, and they (c) . . . . till three or four in the morning. Then there's all the fireworks! All the kids are constantly (d) . . . . bangers, and then there are big (e) . . . . every lunchtime and night. It's awful. I can never get any sleep. I guess it's worth (f) . . . . just once, but personally I can't stand it.

3.

commercial	floats	sound systems	sponsored

Personally, I've stopped going to the Notting Hill Carnival. It's just got too big and too (a) . . . . There are so many people now it's difficult to get close to see the parade. It used to be just a community festival, but now a lot of the (b) . . . . in the parade and a lot of the music stages are (c) . . . . by big businesses. If you are going to go down there, you're best going early on Sunday, when it's a bit quieter, and just hanging out round one of the (d) . . . . which blast out old reggae and ska records.

2 Reacting to good and bad news

Complete the short dialogues below with the pairs of words in the box.

accepted / congratulations
an operation / he's up and about
birthday / returns
Christmas / you
finished / well done
married / congratulations
New Year / same
pregnant / that's great
the doctor's / nothing serious

1. A: I've just . . . . my exams.
   B: Really? . . . .! Are you going to go out and celebrate?

2. A: Bye, and Happy . . . .
   B: Yes, and the . . . . to you.

3. A: It's actually my . . . . today.
   B: Really? Well, many happy . . . . And how old are you, if you don't mind me asking?

4. A: Merry . . . .
   B: Yes, ... too.

5. A: I've just heard I got . . . . on a business management course.
   B: Really? . . . .! When do you start?

6. A: Actually, I'm . . . .
   B: Really? . . . . When's it due?

7. A: Actually, I'm going to . . . . later.
   B: Oh, right. . . . ., I hope.

8. A: He's just had . . . . to sort out his knee. He's at home resting.
   B: Oh, right. Well, send him my best wishes, and I hope . . . . soon.

9. A: I'm getting . . . . in the summer.
   B: Really? . . . .! When's the big day?

3 Relative clauses

In six of these sentences, the relative pronoun is not necessary. Tick if the relative pronoun is necessary. Cross if it is not necessary.

1. I got that stuff that you asked me to get. ☐
2. I got that job that I applied for. ☐
3. I went to that restaurant that we went to for your birthday. ☐
4. I went to that new club that's just opened on George Street. ☐
5. I went to see that film that you were telling me about. ☐
6. He's the kind of person who just won't take no for an answer. ☐
7. She's not the kind of person who you'd want to get stuck in a lift with. ☐
8. She's the kind of person who wouldn't think twice about spending 500 euros on a pair of shoes. ☐
9. She's not the kind of person who would make a fuss. ☐
10. He's the kind of person who you just want to punch. He's so big-headed and full of himself. ☐
11. He's one of those people who never smiles. ☐
12. He's one of those people who always thinks he's right. ☐

4 Relative clauses in questions

Complete the questions below with the relative clauses in the box.

> that's on Channel Four
> which has just opened near you
> you stayed in in Madrid
> you went skiing in
> you went to see last night
> you work for
> you work with
> you're moving to

1. What are the other people . . . . like? ☐
2. What was the hotel . . . . like? ☐
3. What's the company . . . . like? ☐
4. What was the Alpine resort . . . . like? ☐
5. What's the flat . . . . like? ☐
6. What's that bar . . . . like? ☐
7. What was that film . . . . like? ☐
8. What's that new series . . . . like? The one you were telling me about. ☐

Now match the questions 1–8 above to the answers a–h.

a. I don't know. I haven't been in there yet. It looks a bit too trendy for me.
b. It was brilliant. It had a really surprising ending. It really kept you guessing.
c. It was OK, I suppose. I'm glad we weren't there longer. We'd done all the runs after two days.
d. It was a bit of a dump, to be honest. The rooms were really tiny and it wasn't very clean.
e. Great. We get on really well. There's a really nice atmosphere in the office.
f. Great. It's much nicer than our old one – a lot more spacious and a lot brighter.
g. It looks OK. I saw the first episode, but it's on really late.
h. It's OK. It's quite small, but they give us lots of training and support, and so I'm happy there for the moment.

5 Language and speakers

Complete the sentences below with the words in the box.

> accent   jargon   multi-lingual
> bilingual   lingua franca   slang
> dialect   mother tongue

1. Although we're based in Germany, there are people from about five different countries where I work, so we usually use English as a(n) . . . . It's the only language we all have in common.
2. I speak Italian, but when I was in Naples, I found it difficult to follow what people were saying because most people there speak in the local . . . . and a lot of the words and some of the grammar is different.
3. He speaks something like seven languages. He's one of those people who can just pick them up really quickly without really studying. It's really sickening! I wish I was . . . . like that.
4. I'm . . . . because my dad's English and my mum's Spanish, but as I grew up in London I guess you would say English is really my . . . . I sometimes make small mistakes in Spanish.
5. He's very fluent, but he's still got quite a thick Chinese . . . ., so I sometimes don't catch what he's saying.
6. I hate reading these computer manuals. They're so full of . . . ., it's like reading a foreign language.
7. A: What does 'wally' mean? It's not in my dictionary.
   B: Yeah, that's because it's . . . . I think it means 'silly person'. I wouldn't worry about it if I were you. It's not that common and people will probably stop using it after a few years.

6 Talking about language

Complete the sentences below with the words in the box which collocate with *language*.

bad	everyday	offensive	sign
dead	master	official	technical

1. It's really almost impossible to . . . . a foreign language unless you go and live in the country.

2. What I want to learn most is just useful, ... language that people speak.

3. There's no point learning a(n) . . . . language like Latin. No one speaks it these days.

4. English is one of the . . . . languages in my country. It's used as the main language of government.

5. If I can't find the right words when I'm abroad, I just point and move my arms about. I just use . . . . language.

6. My parents don't like me using . . . . language. They've always taught me not to swear.

7. I'm going to have to learn quite a lot of . . . . language when I start writing for this engineering magazine.

8. I hate it when I hear . . . . language like 'You bitch' or people calling foreigners racist names.

Underline the collocations with *language* above.

7 Superlatives

We often use *the* + the superlative form of an adjective to talk about people in the following way:

She's one of the nicest people I know.
She was the most forgetful person I've met.
He must be the ugliest person I've ever seen.

Complete the short dialogues that follow with the superlative form of the adjectives in the box.

arrogant / snobbish	funny
conservative	loud / rude
direct	mean
friendly	quiet

1. A: He's a typical Irishman – really kind and generous!
   B: Yeah, well, they're not all like that. I know this Irish guy and he's . . . . person I've ever met.

2. A: He's a typical Asian student – really quiet and polite.
   B: Yeah, well, they're not all like that. I had this one Chinese student who was one of . . . . and . . . . students I've ever had. He was always shouting out things and interrupting.

3. A: He's a typical Italian guy – really out-going and friendly!
   B: Yeah, well, they're not all like that. I have this Italian friend and he's one of . . . . people I know. He hardly says anything.

4. A: She's a typical American – really liberal and open-minded. You know, anything goes.
   B: Yeah, well, they're not all like that. I stayed in this small town in Iowa and it's one of . . . . places I've ever been in.

5. A: She's a typical Spaniard – really nice and down-to-earth.
   B: Yeah, well, they're not all like that. I used to work for a Spanish guy and he was one of . . . . and . . . . people I've ever met.

6. A: Why are English people so two-faced?
   B: Oh, come on! We're not all like that. I have this friend and she must be . . . . person I know. There are times you wish she would be a little less honest!

7. A: German people – they're just so dull.
   B: Oh, come on! That's such a stereotype. I have this German friend and he's one of . . . . people I know. He's hysterical.

8. A: Why are English people so cold and distant?
   B: Oh, come on! We're not all that bad. Look at me. I'm one of . . . . people you could wish to meet!

Learning tip

It's important to notice the grammar of typical phrases like the ones in Exercise 7. For example, did you notice whether *one of the most + adjective* is followed by *people* or *person*?

Can you see any other grammatical patterns which are repeated in Exercise 7? Try and write your own examples using the same patterns. Check with your teacher to see if they are right.

8 | Countries and nationalities

Complete these sentences with the name of the country.

1. She's Thai. She's from . . . .

2. She's Dutch. She's from some small town in . . . .

3. He's Chinese. He's from mainland . . . . somewhere.

4. She's South Korean. She's from . . . . I think she said she's from Seoul.

5. He's Greek. He's from mainland . . . .

6. He's Cypriot. There are a lot of people who are originally from . . . . near where I live.

7. He's Saudi. He's from . . . ., but he spends a lot of time in London now.

8. His dad's Pakistani. He moved over here from . . . . in the sixties.

9. He's half Swiss, half Spanish. His dad's from . . . . and his mum's from . . . .

10. She's got Argentinian and British dual nationality. Both her parents are actually from . . . ., but she was born in . . . .

9 | Describing your country

Match the comments 1–5 to the follow-up comments a–e.

1. Personally, I'd stay in Penang for a while. It's a very cosmopolitan city. ☐

2. I wouldn't bother going to Donetsk if I were you. It's a very industrial city. ☐

3. You might want to go to Rotterdam. It's a big port. ☐

4. Personally, I wouldn't bother going to Wiltshire. It's a very rural area. ☐

5. I'd definitely go to Krakow. It's a historic town. ☐

a. There's nothing interesting to see there – just mines and factories and a lot of pollution.

b. It's a really interesting place and the old town dates back hundreds of years.

c. It's a really lively place, culturally, and there's a really interesting mix of people.

d. The old harbour's quite nice, and most of the ferries leave from there, but the main part is fairly ugly.

e. It's basically just really dull. When you go through it on the train, it's just mile after mile of fields.

Now match the comments 6–10 to the follow-up comments f–j.

6. If you have time, I'd go to Lanzarote. ☐

7. I wouldn't bother going to Benidorm. It's a big tourist resort. ☐

8. If you like skiing, you might want to go to the Sierra Nevada. It's a very mountainous area, ☐

9. If you can get there, I'd go to Irian Jaya. It's a very remote area. ☐

10. You might want to go to Zaragoza. It's a small provincial city. ☐

f. In the summer, it's full of British people on holiday!

g. so you get snow all the year round.

h. It's really quiet and beautiful. There's not a soul for miles and the transport there can be fairly difficult!

i. It's an island in the Atlantic. It's volcanic. It's really amazing.

j. There's not very much to do there, but the people are very friendly and it's nice to get away from the capital and see other towns.

10 | Where's that, then?

Match each place name to its location on the map.

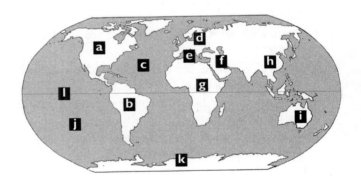

1. The Middle East ☐
2. The Atlantic Ocean ☐
3. North America ☐
4. Africa ☐
5. South America ☐
6. Europe ☐
7. The South Pole ☐
8. The Pacific Ocean ☐
9. The Far East ☐
10. Australia ☐
11. The Mediterranean ☐
12. The Equator ☐

1 Different kinds of crimes

Match the sentences 1–9 to the more detailed follow-up comments a–i.

1. He was found guilty of murder. ☐
2. He was found guilty of vandalism. ☐
3. He was found guilty of rape. ☐
4. He was found guilty of drink driving. ☐
5. He was found guilty of speeding. ☐
6. She was found guilty of possession of drugs. ☐
7. She was found guilty of burglary. ☐
8. She was found guilty of tax evasion. ☐
9. She was found guilty of lying in court. ☐

a. Apparently, he'd had eight pints before setting off!
b. Apparently, she had about half a kilo of cocaine on her when they stopped her.
c. Apparently, he'd smashed up a public phone box and thrown a brick through a bank window.
d. Apparently, she hadn't declared about fifty thousand pounds' worth of her earnings from last year.
e. Apparently, he'd stabbed his brother-in-law sixteen times.
f. Apparently, she'd done it to try and protect her husband.
g. Apparently, he'd forced this woman to have sex with him at knife-point.
h. Apparently, she'd broken into the place next door to her three times!
i. Apparently, he was doing one hundred and thirty when they stopped him.

2 Punishments

Complete the short dialogues about punishments with the words in the box.

community service	poor
death penalty	put other people off
deserved	rich
harsh	throw away
lighter	

1. A: He was unlucky. I thought eight years for car theft was a bit . . . .
   B: I know. I'm surprised he got that many. I was expecting his sentence to be much . . . .

2. A: He should've got life for that!
   B: I know. They should lock people like that up and . . . . the key, not just give them ten years in prison.

3. A: If that'd happened in my country, he would've got the . . . .
   B: I know. People who do things like that deserve the electric chair, if you ask me.

4. A: Ten years sounds about right for what he did.
   B: I know. He definitely got what he . . . .

5. A: Typical! There's one law for the . . . . and another one for the . . . . !
   B: I know. If normal people like you or I had done what he did, we'd have got ten years in prison! There's no justice!

6. A: I think they just decided to try and make an example of him.
   B: I know. I guess they think that giving him thirty years for dealing in drugs will . . . . , but I can't imagine it will.

7. A: He only got a hundred hours' . . . .
   B: I know. All he'll have to do is clean a few walls and help carry a few old ladies' shopping. There's no justice!

3 Number expressions

Complete these sentences with *first*, *second* or *third*.

1. I was planning to go to Bali this summer, but I've been having . . . . thoughts about it since the terrorist attack there.
2. Birmingham's a really great place. It's England's . . . . city.
3. It was love at . . . . sight, it really was. I fell for her the minute I saw her!
4. Don't ask me about things like that. I'm afraid I don't know the . . . . thing about politics!
5. I can't believe I have to give my presentation at eight thirty! I'm useless . . . . thing in the morning.
6. I hate it when people call this a . . . . world country. Why can't they call it a developing country instead?

7. A: I've got my First Certificate exam next month. I'm really dreading it because I've failed twice already.

    B: Oh well, you know what they say – . . . . time lucky!

8. Let's drive round to dad's, shall we? No, hang on. On . . . . thoughts, it'll probably be quicker to get the bus.

9. My . . . . impression of her was that she was a bit selfish, but I've changed my mind a bit since then.

10. I don't think I've ever bought a new car in my life. They've all been . . . . -hand.

Now go back and underline the whole number expressions in the sentences above. Can you translate each one into your own language?

4 Basic crime vocabulary

Match the verbs 1–8 to the words they collocate with a–h.

1. go on	☐	a.	the back door
2. catch	☐	b.	a bank
3. kick in	☐	c.	flats and houses
4. raid	☐	d.	that serial killer
5. burgle	☐	e.	three hundred thousand pounds
6. get away with	☐	f.	the rampage
7. have	☐	g.	someone to death
8. stab	☐	h.	your bag snatched

Now complete the sentences below using the collocations 1–8 above in the correct form. The first one is done for you.

9. A: Did you see the news? They've finally *caught that serial killer*, you know, the one they've nick-named the Beast.

    B: Oh, really? That's great. How many people do they think he's he killed? Eight? Nine?

10. They've charged him with murder. Apparently, he . . . . in a fight in the street.

11. Have you heard the news? Some kid has . . . . in a high school in the States and shot six or seven people.

12. Be careful where you keep your money and your passport and everything. You wouldn't want to . . . . and lose everything, would you?

13. A: My flat got burgled while I was away on holiday. They . . . . and stole my TV and my computer.

    B: Oh, no! That's awful. I'm so sorry.

14. They started off small, just . . . . near where they lived, but eventually, they decided to . . . . and they . . . .

5 Famous and dangerous!

Complete the sentences below with the pairs of verbs in the box.

admitted / got	re-tried / found
caught / kept	went / found
dropped / paid	

1. Jean-Claude van Damme was stopped by the police because he was driving really badly. He . . . . he'd been drinking. He went to court and . . . . fined about one thousand dollars.

2. O.J. Simpson was accused of murder and went on trial, but they found him innocent. Later, though, he was . . . . in a different court and this time I think they . . . . him guilty.

3. Paul McCartney was . . . . trying to smuggle drugs into Japan. They charged him and . . . . him in jail for a few days, but then they let him go.

4. Johnny Depp was arrested after he smashed up a hotel room and was charged with vandalism, but the police . . . . the charges after he . . . . for all the damage.

5. Mike Tyson was charged with rape. He . . . . on trial and was . . . . guilty. He got six years in prison, but they let him out after only three.

Look back at the pairs of verbs in the box above. Can you remember all of the collocations for each pair?

6 Keyword: *crime*

Complete the sentences below with the words in the box.

copycat	juvenile	petty	street
drug-related	organised	sex	war

1. The authorities are worried that the film is so violent, it'll lead to lots of . . . . crimes, where kids commit similar crimes just because they've seen them in the cinema.

2. . . . . crime has become a huge problem. The mafia and the gangs now control whole areas of the city. The big bosses make a fortune from prostitution, money lending, drug-smuggling, and things like that.

3. It's quite rough round the station. There's a real problem with . . . . crime round there – a lot of muggings, that kind of thing.

4. If you ask me, people who commit . . . . crimes against women or young kids should be locked up for life!

5. The former president is now wanted by the UN for . . . . crimes committed during the civil war.

6. There's a real problem now with . . . . crime – kids as young as eleven or twelve are getting involved in shoplifting, mugging, that kind of thing.

7. The police think something like ninety percent of all street crime is . . . . Most muggers and thieves are addicts, desperate to find the money to buy more heroin or cocaine.

8. The police are so busy worrying about terrorism and murders and drugs that they don't really have time to do much about . . . . crime like shoplifting or people breaking into cars.

Now go back and underline all the collocations with *crime*.

7 Third conditionals 1

Match the third conditional sentences 1–5 to the follow-up comments a–e.

1. She was such a great teacher. She really encouraged me to study hard. ☐
2. How was I supposed to know that she was going to be wearing exactly the same dress! ☐
3. But it was real, honestly! It looked just like all the UFOs do in the movies. It was incredible! ☐
4. How was I supposed to know you didn't have to read all the books on the reading list? ☐
5. All you had to do was tell me you needed some help moving house and I would've been there! ☐

a. I wouldn't have believed it if I hadn't seen it with my own eyes!
b. I wouldn't have got into university if it hadn't been for her!
c. I would've done it if you'd asked.
d. If I'd known, I wouldn't have worn it.
e. I wouldn't have done it if I'd known it was optional.

Now match the sentences 6–10 to the follow-up comments f–j.

6. How was I supposed to know how bad the play was going to be? ☐
7. She saved my life! I really thought I was going to die until she pulled me out the river. ☐
8. How was I supposed to know that you were getting married in secret? ☐
9. You know how much I like parties! ☐
10. How was I supposed to know she was already engaged? ☐

f. If you'd told me about it, I would've come.
g. If you'd told me, I wouldn't have mentioned it to a soul!
h. If I'd known, I wouldn't have bothered going.
i. If I'd known, I wouldn't have asked her out!
j. I'm sure I would've drowned if it hadn't been for her.

8 | Third conditionals 2

In Unit 12 of the Coursebook, there is a text about a couple who got arrested for bribing a policeman. This is their conversation in their cell at the police station! Re-read the text in the Coursebook if you like. Complete the dialogue with the correct form of the verbs in brackets. The first one has been done for you.

Nick: This is all your fault! This (1) *wouldn't have happened* (not happen) if you (2) .... (not try) to bribe that policeman!

Jane: Well, if you (3) .... (listen) to me when I suggested asking someone for directions, we (4) .... (not get) lost in the first place, would we?

Nick: Oh, go on! Blame it all on me! You were the one who was driving when we got stopped by the police. If you hadn't been speeding, we (5) .... (not be stop) at all! Then none of this (6) .... (happen).

Jane: That's not fair. If we (7) .... (not take) your stupid short cut, we would've been OK. We were doing fine until you suddenly decided you knew a quicker way! You idiot!

Nick: Oh, come on! I only suggested it because we were running so late. We (8) .... (be) fine if you (9) .... (not suggest) driving instead of taking the train.

Jane: No! We (10) .... (be fine) if *you* (11) .... (remember) to book tickets!

9 | I wish I'd ... / I wish I hadn't ...

When we feel bad about something we did in the past, we often express our regret by using *I wish I hadn't* + past participle. For example:

I wish I hadn't eaten so much earlier. I feel dreadful now!

I wish I hadn't spent so much money while I was in France. I'm totally broke now.

To express our regret about something we now think we should've done in the past, but that we didn't do, we often use *I wish I'd* + past participle. For example:

I wish I'd talked to him when I had the chance. I'll probably never meet him again now!

I wish you'd told me about it. I would've come if I'd known.

Complete these sentences with *I wish I'd* or *I wish I hadn't* and the correct form of the verb in brackets.

1. .... learning English when I was younger! Maybe I would find it easier today. (start)

2. .... on that shopping trip to Singapore last month. I've got two thousand pounds on my visa card now! (go)

3. .... to lift that sofa all on my own! I think I've done something to my back! (try)

4. .... to tape the programme that was on last night. It sounded really good. (remember)

5. .... my grandfather better before he died. He sounded like an amazing old man. (know)

6. .... him about the party. He'll probably bring all his stupid friends along with him now! (tell)

10 | Writing

Complete the e-mail below with the correct form of the verbs in the box.

| cancel | mug | run away | stab |
| jump out | report | shake | threaten |

Dear Freddie,

Well, here I am in the UK. The weather's not too bad. The people are generally quite friendly, but you won't believe this! I got [1] .... on my first day here! It was awful. It was early evening and I was walking back to my hotel along a main road when suddenly two young guys [2] .... in front of me from a doorway and demanded my wallet. I tried to [3] ...., but they grabbed me and [4] .... me with a knife. I was really scared. I thought they were going to [5] .... me, so I handed over all my money, my watch, my credit cards, everything. And then they ran off. I was really badly [6] .... and I was just so shocked that I couldn't really speak for five minutes. Then I realised that there were several other people in the street and nobody had tried to do anything about it. I got really angry and started shouting at everyone! I could've been killed and they were all just standing around, watching. Anyway, I [7] .... it to the police and [8] .... my cards. My dad sent me some money, which was a big help and now I'm just trying to make the most of the rest of my time here. Anyway, I hope you're well.

All the best,

Martin

20 Health

1 Health problems

Complete the short dialogues below with the words in the box.

ankle	hay fever	temperature
back	stomachache	toothache
hangover	strange	

1. A: I've got awful . . . . It's horrible. My nose keeps running, my eyes are watering, and I can't stop sneezing.

   B: Oh, no. Have you tried taking anything for it?

2. A: I've done something . . . . to my knee. It really hurts.

   B: Oh, no. Maybe you should go and see someone about it.

3. A: I think I've got a bit of a(n) . . . . I feel dreadful. I keep getting hot and cold flushes.

   B: Oh, no. Maybe you should take a day off or something.

4. A: I've got a terrible . . . . I think it must've been something I ate. I feel dreadful.

   B: Oh, no. Have you tried taking anything for it?

5. A: I can't run any more. I think I've sprained my . . . . somehow.

   B: Oh, no. Well, maybe you should get the bus back home and just take it easy for a while.

6. A: I had a bit of a late night last night. I've got a bit of a(n) . . . . this morning.

   B: Oh, no. Maybe you should take an aspirin and have a glass of milk or Coke or something. That should help.

7. A: I've got a really bad . . . . I've got to make an appointment with my dentist.

   B: Ouch! Maybe you should take an aspirin or something too, just to kill the pain.

8. A: I've done something strange to my . . . . I can't really stand up straight.

   B: Ouch! Maybe you should go and see someone about it. It could be really nasty.

2 What's the matter?

Put the conversations below into the correct order.

Conversation 1

a. OK, OK. Thanks for the sympathy! ☐

b. What's the matter with you? ☐

c. For a couple of days now. ☐

d. I'm not sure. I think I've got the flu. ☐

e. Well, keep away from me. I don't want to catch anything! ☐

f. Oh, no. How long've you had that? ☐

Conversation 2

a. Well, maybe you should get somebody to give you a massage or something. ☐

b. Yeah, that might be an idea. ☐

c. Are you all right? What happened to your leg? ☐

d. No, it's not that. It's my back. I've done something weird to it. ☐

e. I'm not sure. I just woke up this morning and it was like this. ☐

f. Oh, no. How did you do that, then? ☐

Conversation 3

a. It's my wrist. I think I've sprained it somehow. ☐

b. Oh, no. Well, maybe we should stop playing for a while. ☐

c. Yeah, that might be an idea, actually. ☐

d. It must've been that last shot I played, the back-hand one. ☐

e. Are you OK? ☐

f. Ouch! How did you manage that? ☐

> **Language note**
>
> Did you notice the question *How did you manage that?* in the third conversation? The main meaning of *I managed to* is *it was difficult, but I tried and I did it.* However, we usually use it ironically to talk about stupid things we've done – accidents, mistakes, that kind of thing. Look at these examples:
>
> *How did you manage to break your leg, then?*
> *I'm so stupid! I've somehow managed to leave my passport at home!*

3 Being ironic

Complete the ironic sentences below using *managed* to and the verbs in the box.

burn	forget	lock
cut	get stuck	put
drop	leave	

1. I'm so stupid. I somehow . . . . myself out of my house! I had to jump through a window to get back in.

2. I'm so stupid. I somehow . . . . my wedding ring down the sink! I had to get a plumber to get it out.

3. I can't believe it! I've . . . . the plane tickets at home. I was sure I'd put them in my bag.

4. I couldn't believe it! I somehow . . . . my passport and I had to go all the way back home to get it.

5. She somehow . . . . in the toilet! She couldn't open the door for some reason.

6. He somehow . . . . all the answers to the questions in the wrong spaces. He failed the exam.

7. I . . . . my finger off while I was cooking. I had to go to hospital to have it sewn back on!

8. I . . . . nearly all my hair off while I was lighting the fire! I had to wear a hat for weeks afterwards.

Language note

In English, you don't *forget* something *somewhere*:
Oh no! I've forgotten my money. NOT
I've forgotten my money at home.

If you want to say where, we use the verb *leave*.
Oh, no! I've left my mobile home in the cafe.
Oh, no! I've left my bag on the bus.

4 I'm allergic to it

Complete the sentences describing different kinds of allergies with the words in the box.

dries	shaking	stomachache
itchy	sick	water
rash	sneezes	

1. I think I must be allergic to this kind of soap. Whenever I use it, it really . . . . my skin out.

2. I think I must be allergic to this kind of material. Whenever I wear it, it makes my skin all . . . .

3. I'm allergic to roses. They make my eyes . . . . if I go anywhere near them.

4. I can't wear metal at all. If I do, I get a terrible . . . .

5. I think he must be allergic to work! He starts . . . . every time I suggest that he does any!

6. She's allergic to nuts. If she eats them, she gets a terrible . . . .

7. I can't eat fish at all. If I do, it makes me . . . . It's disgusting!

8. I think he must be allergic to cats. He always . . . . every time he goes near them.

5 Health vocabulary

Match the questions 1–8 to the answers a–h.

1. It's so hot in here. ☐
2. I'm so out of shape. I get out of breath just walking up the stairs! ☐
3. I'm never going to find a girlfriend! It's all because I wear glasses. ☐
4. I wish I could stop smoking. ☐
5. I can't get rid of this cold! I've had it for weeks. ☐
6. I haven't been to the dentist's for ages. ☐
7. I cut my arm open while I was fixing the window. ☐
8. The doctor told me it might be some kind of cancer. ☐

a. Ouch! Did you have to have any stitches?

b. Oh, no! That's awful. That must be really worrying. Are you going to have to have an operation?

c. Well, do you belong to a gym? Because if not, maybe you should join one.

d. I know! I'm surprised no one's fainted yet!

e. Well, why don't you try acupuncture? That's supposed to help you give up, isn't it?

f. Well, why don't you try wearing contact lenses instead?

g. Have you tried taking vitamin pills? They're supposed to good for getting over viruses.

h. Me neither. I really should go and have a check-up. I'm bound to need a filling or something.

6 Things doctors say

Complete the sentences below with the verbs in the box.

breathe	hurt	take
check	pick up	write
give	relieve	

1. Does it .... if I do this?
2. I just need to .... your blood pressure.
3. OK. I'd like you to .... in deeply and out again. Lovely. Thank you.
4. Could you .... your shirt off, please.
5. I'm afraid I'm going to have to .... you a little injection.
6. I'll give you something to .... the pain a little.
7. I'll just .... you out a prescription.
8. You should be able to .... the prescription at any local chemist's.

7 How did you do that, then?

Complete the stories about four accidents with the past simple or past continuous of the verbs in brackets.

1. It happened back when I (a) .... (be) at primary school. One day, I (b) .... (mess around) with some friends and I somehow (c) .... (trip over) and (d) .... (hit) my head on the edge of a table. It (e) .... (be) horrible. I (f) .... (get) this really deep cut just above my eyebrow. There (g) .... (be) blood all over the place. I've still got a bit of a scar there.

2. I (a) .... (play) in the garden, and it (b) .... (be) very muddy, and I (c) .... (slip) and (d) .... (fall) on a piece of broken glass and (e) .... (cut) my hand. There (f) .... (be) blood everywhere, and I burst out crying.

3. I (a) .... (have) a bicycle race with my brother, and we (b) .... (go) round a corner when suddenly, my bike (c) .... (skid) on some gravel, and I (d) .... (fall off). I (e) .... (wear) shorts, and it (f) .... (take) all the skin off my leg. It (g) .... (be) horrible.

4. When I (a) .... (be) about six or seven, I (b) .... (walk) home from the corner shop with my mum, and it (c) .... (be) really cold and icy. My mum (d) .... (slip) and (e) .... (fall over), but because we (f) .... (hold) hands, I (g) .... (fall over) as well. She (h) .... (land) on top of me, and I (i) .... (break) my collar bone!

8 Reporting speech 1

Make reporting sentences by matching the beginnings 1–8 to the endings a–h.

1. I rang them to complain ☐
2. I rang her to invite ☐
3. I rang her to apologise ☐
4. I rang him to see ☐
5. I rang her to try and persuade ☐
6. I rang them to enquire ☐
7. I rang the doctor to ask ☐
8. I rang her to suggest ☐

a. for what I said, but she wouldn't listen and told me to get lost!
b. if he wanted to come over, but he said he's arranged to go out tonight.
c. about the terrible service, but they just gave me the usual list of excuses!
d. about flights, but they said they didn't have any information.
e. him to come to the house, but he told me I'd have to go into the surgery.
f. going to George's for New Year's Eve, but she wants to go somewhere else.
g. her to the party on Friday, but she can't make it.
h. her not to quit her job, but she's already made up her mind.

9 Reporting speech 2

Complete the sentences below with the correct form of the reporting speech verbs in the box.

apologise	invite	suggest
complain	persuade	tell
enquire	see	

1. Look, I've decided already, OK. There's no point trying to .... me to change my mind.
2. I was going to .... about how bad the food was, but I didn't want to make a fuss.
3. Your mum phoned earlier to .... you to make sure you get to her house by nine tomorrow.
4. I .... doing that, but you said you didn't want to.
5. We should really phone Steve and Nick soon and .... them over for dinner.
6. The delivery company called earlier to .... for the delay in sending the parcel!
7. Kathryn phoned for you while you were out to .... if you wanted to meet her and Ella later.
8. Someone called for you earlier to .... about that advert you put in the paper. They said they'll call back later.

10 Keyword: *health*

Complete the sentences below with the words in the box.

farm	inspector	risk
food	insurance	service
good	mental	

1. They had to close the restaurant down because the health . . . . said the kitchen was so dirty, it was dangerous!

2. A lot of the homeless people you see on the streets have . . . . health problems.

3. I don't really like health . . . . that much. Give me a burger and fries any day!

4. My grandmother is amazing. She's eighty-seven and still in really . . . . health.

5. My husband bought me four days at a health . . . . for my birthday. It was really relaxing. Good, fresh food, lots of exercise, lots of massage and saunas – lovely.

6. The health . . . . is still really under-funded. The government should spend more money on it.

7. Most people in America take out private health . . . . in case they ever have to pay doctor's fees or hospital fees.

8. They've closed down the cafe opposite where I work because it's a health . . . . Apparently, they found rats in the kitchen!

11 Giving advice

Complete the sentences giving advice with the structures in the box.

Have you tried	Maybe you should
If I were you	

1. . . . . writing everything down on little cards and sticking them round the house?

2. . . . . take the day off work and get him to a doctor. Better safe than sorry.

3. . . . . changing the battery? That might be what it is.

4. . . . . , I'd stop smoking! You know it's destroying your lungs, don't you?

5. . . . . think about joining a gym or something.

6. . . . . just talking to your landlord about it? I'm sure he'd understand.

12 *Should* for talking about the future

Complete conversations 1–6 with the pairs of words below.

at a conference / tomorrow
at work / sometime early this evening
gone / on Monday
gone / sometime later in the month
just popped out / in a couple of minutes
off sick / next week sometime

1. A: What's happened to Cathy? I haven't seen her for a couple of days.
   B: No. I know. She's . . . . on holiday for three weeks. She should be back . . . .

2. A: Hello. Can I speak to Mr Wilkinson?
   B: I'm afraid he's . . . . this week with the flu. He should be back . . . . Try again next Tuesday or Wednesday.

3. A: Hi. Is Kenny there?
   B: No, he's . . . . to Paris for the weekend. He'll be back . . . . He should be in by nine, if you want to call then.

4. A: Hi. Is Nina there?
   B: No, she's . . . . to the shops. She should be back . . . . Shall I get her to call you back?

5. A: Hello. Can I speak to Mrs Morton, please?
   B: Oh, I'm sorry. I'm afraid she's . . . . today. She'll be back . . . . She should be in around nine.

6. A: Hi. Is your dad there?
   B: No, he's . . . . , I'm afraid. He finishes at around six, so he should be back . . . .

Answer Key

Introduction

1 What is a collocation?
1. lose his memory   2. leave a tip   3. left home
4. missed my train   5. going on holiday   6. doing a degree
7. part-time course   8. save my seat
9. got divorced   10. upset stomach

3 Grammar
1. d.   2. h.   3. a.   4. c.   5. b.   6. e.   7. g.   8. f.

1 Getting to know you

1 Do you like ... ?
1. Yeah, I love it.   2. No, I hate him.   3. No, not really.
4. I've never heard of them.   5. It's all right, I suppose.
6. Yeah, they're OK.

a. 1.   b. 3.   c. 2.   d. 6.   e. 5.   f. 4.

2 How old are they?
1. d   2. e   3. b   4. c.   5. a.   6. g.   7. i.   8. j.
9. h.   10. f.

3 Where is it?
1. b   2. a.   3. b.   4. a.   5. b.   6. a.   7. c.   8. e.   9. d.

4 What's your city like?
1. d.   2. a.   3. e.   4. c.   5. b.   6. g.   7. i.   8. h.
9. j.   10. f.

5 Collocations with *heavy*
1. traffic   2. sleeper   3. smoker   4. film   5. atmosphere
6. night   7. week   8. suitcases   9. lunch   10. conversation

6 Collocations with *question* and *answer*
1. question   2. answer   3. answer   4. answer
5. question   6. answer   7. question   8. question, answer
9. answer, question   10. answer, question

7 Classroom language
1. rub this off, written it all down   2. play, compare
3. borrow, catch up   4. hand out, left   5. toilet, break
6. look through, give

In 1, 4 and 6, it's a teacher speaking first and a student responding.
In 2, 3 and 5, it's a student speaking first, and a teacher responding.

8 Past simple and past continuous
1. I was taking, closed   2. I was rushing, I forgot
3. I didn't recognise, he wasn't wearing   4. I wasn't looking,
I was going, I stepped   5. I wasn't thinking, I was doing,
I pressed   6. I was just getting up, I knocked
7. I was just walking, I caught   8. I didn't see, he was
working

9 Writing: an anecdote
1. once   2. It happened quite a few years ago   3. I was on
holiday   4. I thought I was going to die   5. I'd never do
anything like that again

2 Free time

1 I just stayed in and had an early night
1. I didn't do much last night. I just stayed in and
   watched TV and that was it, really.
2. I didn't eat much this morning – just an apple and a
   piece of toast.
3. It's just a small company. We only employ twelve
   people.
4. I'm just phoning to make sure you got home OK.
5. I'm just writing to say 'Thanks' for the Christmas card
   you sent.
6. No, thanks. I'm just looking.
7. I don't know why you're getting so annoyed about it.
   It was just a silly joke!
8. I'm driving, so could you just get me a Coke, please?

9. d.   10. a.   11. f.   12. b.   13. c.   14. e.

2 Common answers
1. b and e   2. c and i   3. a and h   4. d and j   5. f and g

3 Where do you do that, then?
1. There's a pool near the station that I go to.
2. There's a pitch in the park near my house.
3. There's a court in the park near my house.
4. There's a course on the edge of town that's not too
   expensive.
5. I usually just go round the block a few times.
6. It's held in a community centre near my house.

7. f   8. c.   9. d   10. a.   11. b.   12. e.

4 Expressions of time
1. when I was at university
2. when I was at secondary school
3. when I was about four or five
4. when I was at primary school
5. when I was still a baby
6. not long after I graduated
7. when I was pregnant with our second child
8. when I was studying to go to university
9. when I was about thirty, not long after we got married

The order is: 5, 3, 4, 2, 8, 1, 6, 9, 7

5 How did you get into that?
1. b.   2. d.   3. a.   4. e.   5. c.   6. g.   7. f.

The time expressions are:
1. when I was at school
2. when I was thirteen
3. When I was living in Madrid, not long after I graduated
4. when I was younger
5. When I was at school
6. When I was on holiday in Rome one year
7. when I was at university

6 What's the activity?
1. collecting   2. going swimming   3. going to the gym
4. playing chess

7 What kind of thing is it?
1. a.   2. d.   3. i.   4. g.   5. e.   6. h.   7. b.   8. j.   9. c.
10. f.

8 How long have you been doing that, then?
1. c.   2. e.   3. h.   4. f.   5. b.   6. g.   7. a./g.   8. d.

9 Past simple questions with *How long?*
1. learn, failed   2. stay, left   3. live, ran out of
4. work, job   5. do up, DIY   6. married, split up
7. hospital, operation   8. off work, temperature

10 Asking questions using auxiliary verbs
We make negative questions when the initial sentence is
negative. We use the same auxiliary verb as the initial
statement + *not*. We use *do you* or *did you* when the initial
statement does not have an auxiliary verb in it.

1. Did you?   2. Did you?   3. Have you?   4. Do you?
5. Didn't you?   6. Haven't you?   7. Have you?
8. Are you?   9. Can't you?

3 Holidays

1 Free time
1. weekend   2. day off   3. public holidays
4. on holiday   5. day out   6. long weekend

2 Go + -ing
1. trekking   2. shopping   3. swimming   4. snorkelling
5. sightseeing   6. camping   7. surfing   8. skiing

3 Collocations: *travel, trip, holiday*
1. holiday   2. trip   3. holiday   4. trip   5. travel   6. holiday
7. holiday   8. trip   9. trip   10. travel   11. holiday
12. holiday   13. trip   14. travel   15. holiday   16. holidays
17. holiday   18. Travel

4 Whereabouts are you going?
1. e.   2. h.   3. c.   4. j.   5. a.   6. i.   7. d.   8. b.   9. g.
10. f.

5 Talking about places
1. capital   2. mountain range   3. stream, lake   4. wood
5. states, counties   6. scenery   7. forest   8. river, waterfall
9. hills, views   10. cliff

a. an ocean   b. a forest   c. a mountain   d. a sea
e. a river

6 Answering *Have you been to … ?*
1. supposed   2. wanted   3. sure   4. love   5. when/while
6. to   7. whole   8. 've/have   9. would   10. mine

7 Present perfect and adverbs
1. e.   2. c.   3. g.   4. a.   5. b.   6. i.   7. h.   8. d.   9. f.

The adverbs are: a. just   b. just   c. honestly, already
d. never, really   e. just   f. really   g. actually, already
h. always   i. yet

8 I've just told you!
1. 've just seen   2. 've only just got, has only just started
3. 've only just graduated   4. 've just found out, has just
gone bankrupt   5. 've just done   6. has actually just walked

9 Supposed to be
1. is supposed to be   2. is   3. are supposed to be
4. is supposed to be   5. is supposed to be
6. is   7. is   8. 's supposed to get   9. 's not supposed to be
10. 's   11. is supposed to be   12. 'm supposed to be

10 Writing: a postcard
1. Having   2. Spent   3. architecture   4. couple
5. staying   6. off   7. lying   8. missing

Typical postcard language: 1. g./c.   2. b.   3. a.   4. e.   5. f.
6. d.   7. i.   8. c./g.   9. h.

4 Feelings

1 Starting conversations
1. going   2. Have, waiting   3. What, doing / up to   4. isn't
5. well   6. good / nice   7. mind, join   8. up

1. g.   2. a.   3. e.   4. d.   5. b.   6. c.   7. h.   8. f.

2 How's it going?
1. a, c and d   2. b, g and k   3. e, i and j   4. f, h and l

3 Ending conversations
1.   or I'll be late
2.   or I'll miss my train
3.   or I'll miss the start of the film
4.   or I won't finish this work
5.   or my husband will start to worry
6.   My boyfriend's cooking dinner.
7.   A friend's waiting for me.
8.   I'm meeting a friend of mine at six.
9.   There's a film I want to watch on TV. / There's a
     film on TV I want to watch.
10.   There's a tennis match I want to watch on TV. /
     There's a tennis match on TV I want to watch.

4 Social problems
1. d.   2. a.   3. f.   4. b.   5. e.   6. c.

5 More expressions with get
1. stolen   2. angry   3. late   4. petrol   5. £4.50   6. essay
7. permission   8. details

6 I was surprised!
1. f.   2. d.   3. h.   4. a.   5. c.   6. e.   7. b.   8. g.

a. how   b. number   c. amount

7 Adjectives with two forms
1. disappointed   2. disappointing   3. scary   4. scared
5. exciting   6. excited   7. stressful   8. stressed-out
9. upset   10. upsetting

8 Present continuous: negative responses
1. I'm watching, I'm quite enjoying   2. I'm actually going
round   3. I'm listening to   4. We're having   5. I'm just
reading   6. I'm seeing   7. Are you going, I'm meeting

9 Using the present continuous
1.   I'm just waiting for a friend. We're going out for
     dinner later.
2.   What are you doing now? Do you want to get
     something to eat?
3.   I'm working really, really long hours at the moment.
     It's driving me mad!
4.   I'm meeting Ashley later, if you fancy coming.
5.   What are you doing at the moment? Are you still with
     the same company?
6.   I'm still trying to find a new place to live.
7.   What are you doing now? Are you still studying?
8.   I'm going out later, so I'll phone you when I get back
     home.
9.   We're just going for a coffee over the road if you'd
     like to join us.
10.   I'm living back with my mum and dad now because
     I got evicted from my old place.

10 Explaining present states
1. bankrupt   2. restructured   3. renew   4. fed up with
5. illness   6. break   7. stay   8. the sack   9. quit, re-train

11 In the middle of
1. c.   2. d.   3. b.   4. e.   5. a.   6. i.   7. f.   8. j.   9. g.
10. h.

5 | Work

1 What do you do?
a. sales rep   b. product manager   c. researcher
d. engineer   e. computer programmer   f. marketing
manager   g. sales assistant   h. personnel manager
i. security guard

2 Abbreviations
1. e.   2. d.   3. f.   4. a.   5. c.   6. b.

7. admin, lab   8. CV   9. PA   10. rep   11. IT

3 Have to, don't have to, can
1. f.   2. d.   3. e.   4. b.   5. c.   6. a.   7. k.   8. g.   9. j.
10. l.   11. h.   12. i.

4 I could never get used to that
1. g.   2. b.   3. h.   4. f.   5. e.   6. d.   7. a.   8. c.

5 Conversations about jobs
Conversation 1: c., b., d., a.
Conversation 2: b., d., c., a.
Conversation 3: a., d., b., c.
Conversation 4: f., c., a., d., e., b.

1. What do   2. involve   3. What is, like   4. What are, like
5. What are, you work with like   6. changing jobs?

6 Looking for something else
1. more challenging   2. more rewarding   3. less repetitive
4. better paid   5. less stressful   6. more flexible

7 Must be, must get
a. stressful, tiring, rewarding, upsetting, annoying and great
b. fed up, frustrated, depressed and bored

1. That must be, it is   2. That must be, it can be
3. You must get, I do   4. That must be, it can be
5. You must get, No, not really   6. I do sometimes

8 Work collocations
1. d.   2. b.   3. a.   4. c.   5. g.   6. e.   7. h.   8. f.

9 Writing: a covering letter
1. vacancies   2. part-time   3. As   4. various   5. as well as
6. sole charge   7. knowledge   8. reliable   9. fit in with
10. contact

11. b.   12. g.   13. a.   14. f.   15. c.   16. d.   17. e.

6 | Shopping

1 Shopping collocations
1. brand   2. business   3. market   4. shop   5. product

6. own   7. favourite   8. family   9. profitable   10. street
11. fruit, vegetable   12. betting   13. pet   14. dairy
15. high-tech

2 The best thing is ...
1. c.   2. e.   3. b.   4. d.   5. f.   6. a.   7. j.   8. g.   9. k.
10. h.   11. i.

3 Do you know if there's a chemist's near here?
1. butcher   2. 7–11   3. chemist   4. newsagent   5. art shop
6. bookshop   7. clothes shop   8. the kiosk   9. travel agent
10. fast food restaurant

4 So do I / Neither do I
1. So do I   2. neither do I   3. Neither can I   4. so do I
5. so am I   6. neither have I   7. Neither have I   8. So have I

5 So and *such*
1. so   2. such   3. such   4. so   5. such   6. so   7. such
8. so   9. so   10. such

a. so   b. such

11. cheap   12. expensive   13. good value for money
14. friendly staff   15. dirty   16. tight   17. a nice place to
shop   18. a wide choice   19. unreliable
20. a waste of money

6 Time is money
1a./1b. a bit of a waste of   2a./2b. spent   3a./3b. a bit short
of   4a./4b. worth   5a./5b. save   6a./6b. ran out of
7a./7b. make   8a./8b. Have you got

7 Problems in shops
1. b.   2. a.   3. d.   4. c.   5. g.   6. f.   7. h.   8. e.

8 Things we say in shops
1.   Could you wrap that for me, please?
2.   Could I take two of those, please?
3.   I think I'll leave it for now, thanks.
4.   I might come back for it later.
5.   Could I get it delivered?
6.   Have you got it in a larger size?
7.   Have you got it in any other colours?
8.   Can I try this on somewhere?

9 Supposed to
1. we're not supposed to   2. I'm supposed to   3. we're not
supposed to   4. we're not supposed to   5. we're supposed
to   6. you're not supposed to   7. we're supposed to
8. I'm not supposed to

1. g.   2. e.   3. f.   4. a.   5. h.   6. b.   7. d.   8. c.

7 | Complaints

1 Things we say in hotels
1.   When do you stop serving evening meals?
2.   Have you got any double rooms for three nights?
3.   Is there somewhere safe I could leave these?
4.   Is there somewhere I can park my car overnight?
5.   Is it possible to have breakfast in our rooms, please?
6.   Is it possible to make an international call from my
room?
7.   Is it possible to get these washed and ironed?
8.   Do you think you could order me a taxi into town,
please?
9.   Can I get a wake-up call for six thirty, please?

2 Problems in restaurants
1. b.   2. b.   3. a.   4. b.   5. c.   6. b.   7. c.   8. a.

9. undercooked   10. overcooked   11. knocked over, spilt
12. overbooked   13. rude, leave   14. mixed up   15. accept
16. caught

3 Not very good
1. It doesn't smell very nice
2. didn't look very happy/wasn't looking very happy
3. doesn't taste very sweet
4. I'm not feeling very well
5. doesn't sound very good
6. doesn't taste very dry
7. didn't feel very well
8. don't smell very nice
9. doesn't sound very nice
10. doesn't look very interesting

4 Commenting on what people say
1. That's disgusting 2. That's awful 3. That's a shame
4. That's really annoying 5. That's ridiculous 6. That's hilarious 7. That's brilliant

5 Had to, didn't have to
1. didn't have to 2. had to 3. had to 4. didn't have to
5. had to 6. didn't have to 7. had to 8. didn't have to

6 Excuses
1. had to call, finished 2. had to pop out, got back
3. remembered, had to stay in 4. decided, had to stay in
5. was, had to wait 6. realised, had to go back
7. had to take, had 8. was, had to work

7 It really gets on my nerves!
1. spit, disgusting 2. smoke, killing 3. moan, avoid
4. drives, anti-social 5. racist, black 6. hate, ruins

8 More problems
1. D. 2. C. 3. B. 4. G. 5. H. 6. A. 7. F. 8. E.

9 Writing: a letter of complaint
1. complain 2. compensation 3. delayed 4. board
5. explanation 6. polite 7. possible 8. treated
9. upset 10. refund

10 Using the passive
The ten examples of the passive are: the plane was delayed, we were finally allowed to board, no apology was made, no explanation was offered, we were served them (the in-flight meals), but (I) was told that …, I was reassured that …, the package would be treated with care, but (I) was told that …, there was nothing that could be done

1. g. 2. e. 3. a. 4. h 5. b. 6. c. 7. d. 8. f.

8 House and home

1 Who do you live with?
1. c. 2. d. 3. a. 4. e. 5. b. 6. f.

1. iv. 2. v. 3. ii. 4. i. 5. vi. 6. iii.

2 What's your flat like?
1. spacious 2. cramped 3. bright 4. noisy
5. convenient 6. dark 7. run-down 8. brand new

The negative sentences are: 2, 4, 6 and 7.

3 Was it very expensive?
1. c. 2. e. 3. g. 4. d. 5. a. 6. b. 7. i. 8. f. 9. h.

4 Describing trends
1. have rocketed 2. has fallen dramatically 3. has fallen slightly 4. stayed fairly steady 5. have risen slightly
6. has halved

5 Describing areas 1
1. a. nowhere b. city centre c. lift d. afford e. own
2. a. balcony b. everywhere c. tiny d. noisy e. pain
3. a. rough b. cheap c. share d. cut off e. useless f. fix
4. a. right out b. get away c. fresh air d. dead
e. privacy f. gossiping

6 Describing areas 2
1. h. 2. f. 3. a. 4. g. 5. b. 6. d. 7. c. 8. e.

7 Describing people's bad habits
1. rude 2. unhealthy 3. clumsy 4. immature, childish
5. dishonest 6. mean 7. forgetful 8. boring

8 Housework
1. d. 2. h. 3. a. 4. f. 5. b. 6. c. 7. e. 8. g.

9. sweep the patio
10. hang out the washing/hang the washing out
11. water the plants
12. do the ironing
13. hoover the front room
14. clear the table (after dinner)

9 Collocations with *home* or *house*
1. home 2. home 3. house 4. house 5. house
6. home 7. house 8. home 9. home 10. house
11. house 12. house, house 13. home 14. houses

10 Asking for permission and making requests
1. Do you think you could 2. Is it OK if I 3. Do you think you could 4. Is it OK if I 5. Do you think you could/Is it OK if I 6. Do you think you could 7. Is it OK if I 8. Do you think you could

1. c. 2. f. 3. e. 4. g. 5. d. 6. b. 7. h. 8. a.

9 Computers

1 Your computer
1. disk drive 2. screen 3. file menu 4. icon 5. speaker
6. printer 7. mouse 8. space bar 9. keyboard
10. F-keys

The useful collocations are:
1. double-click on the icon
2. bring up the file menu and then click on …
3. clean the keyboard
4. the screen has frozen
5. the speakers come with the computer, buy the speakers as an add-on
6. use the F-keys
7. The printer has got jammed with paper

2 Talking about computers
1. e-mails 2. file 3. Internet 4. disc 5. system
6. back 7. re-boot 8. online 9. memory 10. laptop

11. check 12. open 13. surfing 14. eject 15. online

3 What software do you use?
1. e. 2. b. 3. d. 4. f. 5. a. 6. c.

4 Computers – love them or hate them?
1. keep in touch 2. look things up 3. book 4. the news
5. send 6. banking 7. can't stand 8. junk e-mails
9. deleting 10. order

5 Have you ever … ?
1. been 2. felt 3. tried 4. seen 5. heard 6. been
7. had 8. fallen

1. h. 2. a. 3. c. 4. f. 5. e. 6. g. 7. b. 8. d.

6 Superlatives with the present perfect
1. worst meal I've had
2. best gigs I've ever been to
3. poshest (place/hotel) I've ever stayed in
4. most boring men I've ever met
5. funniest people I've ever met
6. most enjoyable night out I've had
7. worst film I've ever seen
8. best books I've ever read
9. saddest thing I've heard
10. most disgusting thing I've seen

7 Replying to advice
1. d, b, a and c 2. d, c, b and a 3. c, d, a and b
4. b, a, d and c

8 Responding to advice
1. success 2. hint 3. work 4. good 5. do 6. help
7. suggest 8. one

9 Keep + -ing
1. forgetful 2. polite 3. aggressive 4. bossy 5. nosy
6. naughty

10 Collocations with mistake
1. spelling 2. makes, learn from 3. took 4. discover
5. made 6. expensive 7. biggest 8. admit

The useful collocations are:
1. This letter is full of spelling mistakes
2. Everybody makes mistakes, learn from your mistakes
3. I took it home by mistake
4. They didn't discover their mistake until …
5. I made the mistake of …
6. It was quite an expensive mistake
7. it'll be the biggest mistake of their lives
8. admit you've made a mistake

11 Writing: e-mails
1. e. 2. b. 3. a. 4. f. 5. d. 6. c.

7. arranged 8. last 9. add 10. e-mail
11. Look forward to

10 Meeting people

1 Sorry I'm late
1. i. 2. g. 3. j. 4. b. 5. a. 6. d. 7. e. 8. c. 9. f.
10. h.

2 Keyword: main
1. road 2. tourist area 3. entrance 4. thing 5. difference
6. line 7. course 8. reason 9. meal 10. square

3 Using the infinitive to express purpose
1. j. 2. d. 3. a. 4. b. 5. i. 6. e. 7. g. 8. c. 9. h.
10. f.

4 A night out
Restaurant: book a table, catch the waiter's eye, have a
starter, leave the waiter a tip, they serve big portions

Cinema: book tickets, sit in the back row, eat some
popcorn, watch the trailers before the film, the film has
subtitles

Theatre: book a seat, sit in the stalls, buy a programme, have
an interval of fifteen minutes, give the actors a standing
ovation

5 Arranging to meet
1. let you know 2. the plan 3. arranged 4. was
wondering if 5. on the safe side 6. get ready
7. I'm wrong 8. where I mean

6 I'm just phoning to …
1. meet up, I'm afraid 2. OK for, forgotten 3. see, going
away 4. come over, What time 5. house-warming party,
moved 6. cancelled, relief 7. remember, reminding
8. check, much better

7 I'm not bothered
1. I can't be bothered 2. I wouldn't bother if I were you
3. Sorry to bother you 4. it doesn't bother me
5. I don't bother 6. Don't bother 7. I'm not bothered

8 Adding extra comments
1. e. 2. d. 3. a. 4. h. 5. b. 6. g. 7. c. 8. f.

9 Verb patterns
1. persuade, refusing 2. offered, insisted 3. avoiding 4. get
used to 5. fancy 6. let 7. regret, warn 8. to come,
staying 9. being 10. buying 11. having 12. to pay, to talk
13. to avoid travelling 14. get

10 Do you want to …, or shall we …?
1. e. 2. c. 3. d. 4. f. 5. a. 6. b.

11 Transport and travel

1 Cars
1. engine 2. windscreen 3. mirror 4. back window
5. boot 6. door 7. tyre 8. indicator

2 Tend to
1. tend to go 2. tend not to go/don't tend to go
3. tend to do, tends to do 4. tend to be
5. tend not to leave/don't tend to leave 6. tend to be
7. tended to be 8. tended not to eat/didn't tend to eat

3 How did it happen?
1. f. 2. h. 3. a. 4. g. 5. c. 6. b. 7. d. 8. e.

9. go through 10. corner 11. avoid 12. skid 13. without
14. cut 15. back 16. do

4 Comparing now with the past
1. more 2. polite 3. higher 4. more 5. clean
6. dangerous 7. lower 8. easier 9. more
10. drug addicts

5 Fixed comparative phrases
1. f. 2. d. 3. b. 4. a. 5. c. 6. e.

6 More comparatives
1. more quickly 2. more often 3. more carefully 4. more
smoothly 5. harder 6. faster 7. worse, worse 8. better

7 Nightmare journeys
1. d. 2. b. 3. a. 4. g. 5. f. 6. c. 7. e.

8 Collocations with rough
1. a good night's sleep 2. somewhere cleaner and safer
3. much better 4. write it up more neatly 5. smooth
6. calmer 7. know exactly 8. somewhere with better
discipline

The collocations with *rough* are:
1. have a rough night   2. a rough area   3. feel a bit rough
4. write something in rough   5. the rough side
6. the ferry crossing was rough   7. at a rough guess
8. a rough school

9 What a stupid thing to do!
1. f.   2. d.   3. e.   4. b.   5. a.   6. c.

1, 2 and 5 were driving.   4 and 6 were flying.
3 was taking the train.

10 Writing: connecting ideas
So links two clauses in the middle of a sentence. It shows the reason for something. It comes after a comma.

Then usually comes at the start of a sentence and is followed by a clause to simply show what you did next. If it's in the middle of a sentence, we use *and then*.

Because of has the same meaning as *because* but is followed by a noun/*-ing* form.

By the time usually comes at the start of a sentence and is followed by a clause – often *by the time we got there* – to show something happened before you arrived somewhere.

Despite usually comes at the start of a sentence or a clause and is followed by a noun/*-ing*. It contrasts two facts.

But usually comes in the middle of a sentence followed by a clause. We usually put a comma before *but*.

Though means *but*. It usually comes at the end of a sentence/clause, after a comma.

Because usually links two clauses and shows the reason why. It can go at the beginning of a sentence or in the middle.

1. though   2. Despite   3. By the time   4. Then   5. because of   6. Because   7. so   8. but

12 Food

1 It's a kind of ...
1. F.   2. G.   3. C.   4. H.   5. B.   6. A.   7. D.   8. E.

1. vi.   2. iii.   3. ii.   4. v.   5. vii.   6. viii.   7. i.   8. v.

2 Too and enough
1. too   2. enough   3. too   4. too   5. enough   6. enough
7. enough   8. too

3 There's too much / There are too many
1. There's too much   2. There's too much
3. There are already too many   4. There's already too much
5. There are too many   6. There are too many
7. There are too many   8. There's already too much

4 Keyword: food
1. left over   2. dog   3. junk   4. organic   5. foreign   6. fast
7. genetically-modified   8. health

9. h.   10. e.   11. a.   12. b.   13. c.   14. d.   15. g.   16. f.

5 Food vocabulary
1. a. lost   b. put on   c. going on
2. a. junk   b. organic   c. health
3. a. rotten   b. ripe   c. green   d. tinned
4. a. lovely   b. heavy   c. main   d. light
5. a. balanced   b. special   c. health   d. raw

6 It should be banned
1. g.   2. a.   3. f.   4. h.   5. d.   6. b.   7. e.   8. c.

7 Eating vocabulary
1. starter, main course   2. lunch   3. snacks   4. barbecue, picnic   5. takeaway   6. side dish   7. dessert   8. brunch

8 Eating out in a big group
1. starter   2. selection   3. portions   4. shout   5. allergic
6. rather   7. hands up   8. house wine   9. main course
10. go for   11. good   12. ready

9 More questions you might ask in a group
1. Has anyone got enough room left for dessert or is everyone full already?
2. Does anyone want a coffee?
3. Has anyone asked for the bill?
4. Are we just going to split the bill?
5. Is anyone good at maths?
6. How much is it for each person?
7. Does that include a tip?
8. We're still short twenty euros.

10 Should've / shouldn't have
1. shouldn't have   2. should've   3. shouldn't have
4. should've   5. shouldn't have   6. shouldn't have
7. should've   8. shouldn't have   9. should've   10. should've

13 Sightseeing

1 Places to visit
1. g.   2. e.   3. b.   4. a.   5. h.   6. c.   7. d.   8. f.

9. a cathedral   10. a science museum   11. a jazz club
12. a Hindu temple   13. a portrait gallery   14. a theme park   15. an arts and crafts market   16. a travelling funfair

2 What's it like?
Conversation 1: a. like   b. rip-off   c. miss   d. know
Conversation 2: a. arcade   b. trap   c. give   d. letting
Conversation 3: a. bargains   b. visit   c. telling   d. chance

3 Questions and answers
1. Do you take euros here?
2. Do you think you could take a photo for us?
3. Do you know if this is the way to the Guggenheim museum?
4. Are there any places left on the guided tour?
5. Are there any tickets left for the concert tonight?
6. Have you got any rooms available?
7. Could you help me? I've just had my bag stolen.

1. e.   2. d.   3. b.   4. g.   5. a.   6. c.   7. f.

4 Weather vocabulary
1. miserable, soaked   2. stopped, easing off   3. raining, pouring down   4. cloud over, sunny   5. cloudy, brighten up
6. hot, get up to   7. snow, last   8. cold, gets   9. mild, drops
10. Unbearable, sticky

5 I don't know
1. I've no idea.   2. I haven't really decided yet.
3. I'm still not very sure.   4. I'm still in two minds about it.
5. I haven't really thought about it.   6. I can't make up my mind.

6 'll / going to / might
Conversation 1: a. 'll   b. 'm going to   c. are you going to   d. might
Conversation 2: a. are you going to   b. 'm going to
c. 'll/might   d. might/'ll   e. 'll   f. 'll
Conversation 3: a. 'm going to   b. 'll   3. 'll   4. might

7 Future expressions
1. Wednesday the 14th 2. Tuesday the 27th 3. Saturday the 17th 4. Tuesday the 20th 5. Friday the 23rd 6. Monday the 26th

8 I might … if …
1. f. 2. a. 3. b. 4. g. 5. d. 6. c. 7. e.

9 It depends
1a. on 1b. if /whether 2a. when/what time 2b. how 3a. how much 3b. how long 4a. if/whether 4b. how

10 Writing: I was wondering
1. if I could come and visit 2. if you could put me up 3. if you haven't got space 4. if you're not going to be around 5. if there's some other problem 6. whenever you can

1. f. 2. d. 3. e. 4. a. 5. b. 6. c.

14 Studying

1 School subjects
1. RE 2. physics 3. PE 4. IT 5. biology 6. art 7. maths 8. history 9. geography 10. chemistry

a. IT b. history c. art d. maths e. biology f. RE g. geography h. chemistry i. physics j. PE

2 The worst teacher I ever had!
1. never 2. never 3. always 4. always 5. never 6. always 7. always 8. never 9. never 10. always

3 Punishments
1. got caught 2. skipping 3. given lines 4. humiliating 5. detention 6. bad fight 7. suspended 8. expelled

4 Verb patterns
1. to me about the mess in the kitchen 2. for being drunk at work 3. stealing a book from the library 4. me for the incident 5. to shoot me 6. playing 7. me swear not to tell anyone 8. me with the sack 9. teachers for children's bad behaviour 10. travelling without a ticket 11. for sexually harassing his secretary 12. to the school several times about our teacher

5 How did your exam go?
1. messed 2. revision 3. mind 4. scraped 5. Most 6. None 7. expecting 8. cheating 9. re-taking 10. passed

6 How did it go?
1. exam, OK, I think 2. interview, Terribly 3. class, Great 4. meeting, Don't ask 5. driving test, Great 6. meeting, Great 7. interview, Really well 8. class, OK

7 Studying at university
1. a. finals b. essays c. term d. presentation e. tutorial
2. a. dissertation b. deadline c. lectures d. handouts
3. a. grant b. fees c. options d. specialise e. coursework

8 What are you studying?
a. engineering b. design c. history d. studies

1. graphic 2. civil 3. mechanical 4. media 5. product 6. ancient 7. business 8. modern 9. African

9 Tests and exams
1. c. 2. a. 3. b. 4. h. 5. g. 6. e. 7. d. 8. f.

10 Plans and hopes
1. g. 2. d. 3. b. 4. f. 5. a. 6. e. 7. c.

11 Short natural answers
1. It'll probably 2. I doubt it 3. Hopefully 4. I doubt it 5. I might 6. Probably 7. Hopefully 8. Hopefully not

15 Sport

1 Do, play or go?
1. going 2. play 3. playing 4. do 5. going 6. doing 7. play 8. go 9. play 10. going 11. does 12. goes 13. do 14. playing 15. doing

2 Are you any good?
1. b. 2. g. 3. h. 4. e. 5. f. 6. c. 7. a. 8. d.

3 Win or beat?
1. win 2. beat 3. win 4. beat 5. beat 6. win 7. win 8. beat 9. win 10. beat 11. win 12. beat

13. time 14. rivals 15. competition 16. record 17. champions 18. set

4 Different kinds of games
1. cup 2. computer 3. team 4. card 5. drinking 6. board 7. away 8. ball 9. season 10. kids'

5 More first conditionals
Conversation 1: a. won't be able to b. does c. 'll be able to d. doesn't e. 'll be
Conversation 2: a. will she be able to b. does c. 'll work something out d. 'll be e. stays
Conversation 3: a. 'll be b. does c. 'll be d. 'll meet e. 'll have to f. 'll probably give
Conversation 4: a. 'll ruin b. does c. won't get d. 's not e. drops out f. will she pay g. 'll find

6 Expressions with if
1. tell 2. see 3. give 4. might 5. rather 6. hand 7. don't 8. let

a. if I hear the result, I'll give you a ring b. I'll give you a hand if you want c. I'll tell her if I see her d. I'll see if I can e. I might do it later if I feel like it f. I'll let you have it if I can find it g. I'll go if I really have to, but I'd rather not h. We don't have to buy it if you don't like it

7 He should've scored that!
1. e. 2. b. 3. d. 4. a. 5. c. 6. g. 7. i. 8. j. 9. f. 10. h.

8 I know / I don't know
1. I don't know 2. I know 3. I know 4. I know 5. I don't know 6. I don't know 7. I don't know 8. I don't know 9. I know 10. I don't know

9 Writing
1. 1. told 2. interested 3. wondering 4. exact 5. run 6. recommended 7. keen 8. available 9. grateful 10. necessary

16 Business

1 What kind of business?
1. multinational 2. family 3. myself 4. firm 5. provides 6. designing 7. specialises 8. sells 9. exporting 10. producing

2 Problems, problems!
1. getting worse, deal with 2. caused 3. sort out 4. ignoring

3 More problems
1. marital   2. health   3. mental health   4. social   5. financial
6. technical   7. admin   8. behavioural

4 Collocations: *company* and *business*
1. do   2. partner   3. losing   4. car   5. design   6. policy
7. news   8. keep   9. good   10. mind

7, 8, 9 and 10 are all idioms. You may have completely different ways of saying these in your language; ways which don't use the words *company* or *business*.

5 How's business?
1. Bad   2. Just OK   3. Great   4. Great   5. Bad   6. Just OK
7. bad   8. great   9. Just OK   10. Great   11. Great   12. Bad
13. Bad   14. Great

a. *this year, so far, recently* and *since last year* go with the present perfect   b. *at the moment* goes with present continuous   c. *in the next year* and *over the next year* go with *going to*

6 Business verbs
1. a. withdraw   b. launched   c. modified   d. re-launched
2. a. reduced   b. raised   c. received   d. re-think   e. set
3. a. chose   b. started   c. interrupt   d. develop
e. wrecked

7 Important expressions
1. risen   2. housing   3. reduce   4. weak   5. schools
6. increase   7. recession   8. petrol

8 Promises, promises
1. d.   2. c.   3. b.   4. a.   5. g.   6. h.   7. e.   8. f.

1. viii.   2. i.   3. vii.   4. iv.   5. vi.   6. v.   7. iii.   8. ii.

9 First and second conditionals
1. did, I'd have to   2. I wouldn't go out, was   3. get, I'll start   4. did, I'd go   5. I'd lend, could   6. is, I'll stay in
7. I'd be, did   8. I'll ring, get   9. wouldn't do, paid
10. did, would ignore

10 Grammar: *would* or *'ll*
1. 'll   2. would   3. 'll   4. 'll   5. would   6. would
7. would   8. 'll   9. would   10. 'll   11. would   12. 'll

17 Friends and family

1 Relationships
1. niece   2. ex   3. cousins   4. half-brother
5. mother-in-law   6. nephew   7. step-brother

8. c   9. e   10. a   11. b   12. f   13. d.

2 Adjectives and expressions to describe people
1. strict, lets   2. liberal, let   3. gorgeous, looks   4. fussy, please   5. quiet, says   6. independent, get   7. big-headed, showing off   8. outgoing, get on with

3 Know, get to know, meet, make, have
1. a. know   b. have only known   c. know
2. a. get to know him   b. got to know   c. got to know
3. a. have you met   b. to meet/meeting   c. met
d. 'm meeting   e. met   f. met
4. a. make   b. haven't really made   c. have   d. have   e. is
f. be

4 Present perfect and past simple
1. I've known her   2. I've known her   3. I met her   4. I've known her   5. I met her   6. I met her   7. I've known her
8. I met her

5 Relationship verbs
1. e.   2. b.   3. a.   4. f.   5. c.   6. d.

6 Second conditionals
1. 'd never say   2. 'd never do   3. 'd never go out, looked
4. 'd never go out, treated   5. 'd tell, did   6. took, 'd dump   7. 'd do, found out, 'd probably just try   8. 'd do, left, 'd probably have   9. 'd do, happened, 'd probably go mad   10. found out, was, 'd faint

7 Guessing and being vague
1. think   2. seems   3. a bit   4. reckon   5. must   6. wonder
7. can't   8. must   9. something to do with   10. some kind of

8 Talking about recent history
1. a big recession   2. a civil war   3. independence
4. in power   5. a social revolution   6. a huge economic boom   7. the end of the cold war   8. a dictatorship
9. a very exciting time

9 I used to, but I don't any more
1. f.   2. h.   3. a.   4. b.   5. c.   6. g.   7. d.   8. e.

10 Writing: describing social trends
1. a recent report   2. over the next ten years   3. a number of factors   4. over the last few years   5. significant
6. continue

7. according to   8. will need   9. due to   10. has declined
11. rise   12. continue to

18 Nationalities, festivals and languages

1 Festivals
1. a. street party   b. fantastic parade   c. bands
d. outrageous costumes
2. a. is on   b. outdoor concerts   c. go on   d. letting off
e. firework displays   f. going to
3. a. commercial   b. floats   c. sponsored   d. sound systems

2 Reacting to good and bad news
1. finished, Well done   2. New Year, same   3. birthday, returns   4. Christmas, you   5. accepted, Congratulations
6. pregnant, That's great   7. the doctor's, Nothing serious
8. an operation, he's up and about   9. married, Congratulations

3 Relative clauses
The relative pronoun is not needed in 1, 2, 3, 5, 7 and 10.

4 Relative clauses in questions
1. you work with   2. you stayed in in Madrid   3. you work for   4. you went skiing in   5. you're moving to   6. which has just opened near you   7. you went to see last night
8. that's on Channel Four

1. e.   2. d.   3. h.   4. c.   5. f.   6. a.   7. b.   8. g.

5 Language and speakers
1. lingua franca   2. dialect   3. multi-lingual   4. bilingual, mother tongue   5. accent   6. jargon   7. slang

6 Talking about language
1. master   2. everyday   3. dead   4. official   5. sign   6. bad
7. technical   8. offensive

7 Superlatives
1. the meanest   2. the loudest and rudest   3. the quietest
4. the most conservative   5. the most arrogant and snobbish   6. the most direct   7. the funniest   8. the friendliest

8 Countries and nationalities
1. Thailand 2. Holland/the Netherlands 3. China 4. South Korea 5. Greece 6. Cyprus 7. Saudi Arabia 8. Pakistan 9. Switzerland/Spain, Spain/Switzerland 10. Argentina/Britain, Britain/Argentina

9 Describing your country
1. c. 2. a. 3. d. 4. e. 5. b. 6. i. 7. f. 8. g. 9. h. 10. j.

10 Where's that, then?
1. f. 2. c. 3. a. 4. g. 5. b. 6. d. 7. k. 8. j. 9. h. 10. i. 11. e. 12. l.

19 Law and order

1 Different kinds of crimes
1. e. 2. c. 3. g. 4. a. 5. i. 6. b. 7. h. 8. d. 9. f.

2 Punishments
1. harsh, lighter 2. throw away 3. death penalty 4. deserved 5. rich, poor 6. put other people off 7. community service

3 Number expressions
1. second 2. second 3. first 4. first 5. first 6. third 7. third 8. second 9. first 10. second

The expressions are:
1. I've been having second thoughts 2. is (England's) second city 3. It was love at first sight 4. I don't know the first thing about (politics) 5. first thing in the morning 6. a third world country 7. third time lucky 8. On second thoughts 9. My first impression of (her) 10. second-hand

4 Basic crime vocabulary
1. f. 2. d. 3. a. 4. b. 5. c. 6. e. 7. h. 8. g.

9. caught that serial killer 10. stabbed someone to death 11. gone on the rampage 12. have your bag snatched 13. kicked in the back door 14. burgling flats and houses, raid a bank, got away with three hundred thousand pounds

5 Famous and dangerous!
1. admitted, got 2. re-tried, found 3. caught, kept 4. dropped, paid 5. went, found

6 Keyword: crime
1. copycat 2. Organised 3. street 4. sex 5. war 6. juvenile 7. drug-related 8. petty

7 Third conditionals 1
1. b. 2. d. 3. a. 4. e. 5. c. 6. h. 7. j. 8. g. 9. f. 10. i.

8 Third conditionals 2
1. wouldn't have happened 2. hadn't tried 3. 'd listened 4. wouldn't have got 5. wouldn't have been stopped 6. would've happened 7. hadn't taken 8. would've been 9. hadn't suggested 10. would've been fine 11. had remembered

9 I wish I'd ... / I wish I hadn't ...
1. I wish I'd started 2. I wish I hadn't gone 3. I wish I hadn't tried 4. I wish I'd remembered 5. I wish I'd known 6. I wish I hadn't told

10 Writing
1. mugged 2. jumped out 3. run away 4. threatened 5. stab 6. shaken 7. reported 8. cancelled

20 Health

1 Health problems
1. hay fever 2. strange 3. temperature 4. stomachache 5. ankle 6. hangover 7. toothache 8. back

2 What's the matter?
Conversation 1: b., d., f., c., e. and a.
Conversation 2: c., d., f., e., a. and b.
Conversation 3: e., a., f., d., b. and c.

3 Being ironic
1. managed to lock 2. managed to drop 3. managed to leave 4. managed to forget 5. managed to get stuck 6. managed to put 7. managed to cut 8. managed to burn

4 I'm allergic to it
1. dries 2. itchy 3. water 4. rash 5. shaking 6. stomachache 7. sick 8. sneezes

5 Health vocabulary
1. d. 2. c. 3. f. 4. e. 5. g. 6. h. 7. a. 8. b.

6 Things doctors say
1. hurt 2. check 3. breathe 4. take 5. give 6. relieve 7. write 8. pick up

7 How did you do that, then?
1. a. was b. was messing around c. tripped over d. hit e. was f. got g. was
2. a. was playing b. was c. slipped d. fell e. cut f. was
3. a. was having b. were going c. skidded d. fell off e. was wearing f. took g. was
4. a. was b. was walking c. was d. slipped e. fell over f. were holding g. fell over h. landed i. broke.

8 Reporting speech 1
1. c. 2. g. 3. a. 4. b. 5. h. 6. d. 7. e. 8. f.

9 Reporting speech 2
1. persuade 2. complain 3. tell 4. suggested 5. invite 6. apologise 7. see 8. enquire

10 Keyword: health
1. inspector 2. mental 3. food 4. good 5. farm 6. service 7. insurance 8. risk

11 Giving advice
1. Have you tried 2. Maybe you should 3. Have you tried 4. If I were you 5. Maybe you should 6. Have you tried

12 Should for talking about the future
1. gone, sometime later in the month 2. off sick, next week sometime 3. gone, on Monday 4. just popped out, in a couple of minutes 5. at a conference, tomorrow 6. at work, sometime early this evening